All About
the Love of Food

Janie Ebinger

MOUNTAIN ARBOR
PRESS

Mountain Arbor
PRESS
Alpharetta, GA

ISBN: 978-1-63183-125-6

10 9 8 7 6 5 4 3 2   0 7 1 3 1 7

Printed in the United States of America

⊗This paper meets the requirements of ANSI/NISO Z39.48-1992 (Permanence of Paper)

Cover design by Gabe Vogelsong of Rogue Art Tattoo, New Haven, Indiana
Photography by Janie Ebinger, Mitzi Yvonne Muzzillo Hilkey, and Lisa Koehl-Myers

Dedication

I am dedicating this recipe book, *All About the Love of Food*, in memory of my beloved cousin Charles "Chuck" Martin Russell Jr. and his girlfriend, Catherine "Cathy" Nelson. They left us much too early in life, and we will never stop missing them.

Thank you Barbara and Lonnie Cox, founders of Shepherd's House in Fort Wayne, Indiana, for your love and support of our veterans and civilian men in need of love and direction. I also want to thank Mad Anthonys Children's Hope House on the campus of Lutheran Hospital in Fort Wayne, Indiana, for all the support and love they give to the families of children and other members of their families that are patients in Lutheran Hospital or any hospital in Fort Wayne. This is a beautiful home where the families stay for as long as it is needed, free of charge if they cannot afford the ten-dollar nightly fee. No one is ever turned away, because if they do not have ten dollars, the cost if forgiven.

I also want to give my thanks to God, our Lord and Savior. Without this desire and talent to create these recipes he has given me, I would not be writing this book, *All About the Love of Food*, and the other three I have written: *Simply Vinaigrettes: From Ancho Chili to White Wine*, *Janie's Simply Entree Salads for Two*, and *Live Well Eat Well: Janie's Twist on Salads, Sandwiches, and Wraps*.

Contents

Acknowledgments .... *xiii*
Introduction .... *xv*

Cooking Terms and Meanings .... *xvii*
Measurements, Abbreviations, and Equivalents .... *xix*
Oven Temperatures .... *xxi*

Appetizers

Filo-Wrapped Brie with Almonds,
Raspberries, and Balsamic Drizzle (V) 2
Wild Mushrooms in Filo Cups (V) 4
Shrimp-Filled Filo Cups with Lemongrass-
Mint Balsamic and Toasted Sesame Seed Oil 6
Stuffed Mushrooms 8
Buffalo Spinach Artichoke Dip (V) 10
Antipasti Display 12
Grilled Fruit Kabobs (V) 14
Vegetable Kabobs (V) 16
Duck and Fruit Kabobs 17
Brie in Puff Pastry with Pecan Pesto (V) 19
    Pecan Pesto (V) 22
    Crostini (V) 23

Soups

Italian Bean 26
Stock 28
Broth 30
Hearty Tomato (V) 31
Spinach (Florentine) Chicken 32
Cream of Chicken Noodle 33
    Chicken Broth 34
    Béchamel Sauce (V) 35
Asian Chicken 36
Chicken Enchilada 38
Black Bean 39
Turkey Vegetable 41
Hearty Beef and Tomato 42

Vinaigrettes

Grape Bacon _____ 45
Roasted Red Bell Pepper El Pato (V) _____ 46
Fat-Free and/or Sugar-Free Mixed Berry (V) _____ 47
Apple Maple Cayenne Pepper (V) _____ 48
Bacon Avocado _____ 49
Tomato Mint (V) _____ 50
Rhubarb (V) _____ 51
Strawberry Chipotle (V) _____ 52
Fat-Free Dried Fruit (V) _____ 53
Mirin Red Onion (V) _____ 54
Smoked or Roasted Red Onion Red Bell Pepper (V) ____ 55
Red Onion Strawberry (V) _____ 57
Tomato Roasted Garlic Chive (V) _____ 58
Fat-Free Canned Fruit (V) _____ 59
Roasted Garlic (V) _____ 60
Fat-Free Blackberry Cranberry (V) _____ 61
Strawberry Blueberry Chocolate (V) _____ 63
Spicy Blueberry Sweet Italian (V) _____ 64
Pineapple Horseradish (V) _____ 65
Roasted Nectarine Green Onion (V) _____ 66
Citrus Red Onion Tarragon (V) _____ 67
Spicy Thousand Island _____ 68
Strawberry Coconut (V) _____ 69
Apple Fig (V) _____ 70
Strawberry Pear Red Onion (V) _____ 71
Pumpkin (V) _____ 72
Chocolate-Covered Cherry Cordials (V) _____ 73
Chocolate-Covered Blueberry Cordials (V) _____ 74
Pomegranate Balsamic and Almond EVOO (V) _____ 75
Raspberry Chocolate Balsamic (V) _____ 76
Pineapple Tomato Tarragon (V) _____ 77

Dinners and Entree Salads

Grape Bacon Banana _____ 81
Apple Maple Cayenne Pepper Chicken _____ 82
Spinach Avocado Chicken _____ 83
Tomato Mint _____ 84
Pork and Berries _____ 86
Nectarine Walnut (V) _____ 87

Citrus Apple Pear 88
Grilled Vegetables (V) 89
Green Tomatoes, Berries, and Almonds 90
Strawberry Banana Coconut 92
  Breaded Chicken Strips 93
Strawberry Pear 94
Pumpkin Candied Bacon 96
  Pumpkin-Spiced Candied Bacon 97
  Pumpkin-Spiced Candied Pecans 98
  Pumpkin Spice Croutons 99
Baby Greens and Tomato with
Pomegranate Balsamic and Almond EVOO 100
Chocolate-Covered Cherry Cordials (V) 101
Raspberry Chocolate 102

Sandwiches, Roll-Ups, Wraps, and Flatbreads

Four-Cheese Panini 104
Tomato Ricotta Cheese Hoagie 105
Italian Meats and Cheeses Roll-Ups 106
Fruit, Berry, and Vegetable Wrap (V) 107
Strawberry Chipotle Chicken Wrap 108
Pork Pineapple Horseradish Wrap 109
Fork-and-Knife Flatbread Ham and Egg 110
Mozzarella Tomato Berries Chicken Flatbread 111
Spinach Pesto Flatbread 113
  Spinach Pesto 114

Sauces and Au Jus

Rhubarb Sauce (V) 116
Roasted Garlic Cream Sauce (V) 117
Roasted Red Bell Pepper Sauce (V) 119
Mushroom Au Jus 120
Mushroom Beef Sauce 121
Beef Gravy 122
Chicken Dijon Sauce 123
Cherry Sauce (V) 124
Swedish Meatball Sauce (V) 125
Green Tomato Sauce 126
Mornay Sauce (V) 128

Relishes and Condiments

Sauerkraut Relish (V) _____131
Olive Relish (V) _____132
Green Relish (V) _____133
Icebox Pickles (V) _____134
Mustard Cauliflower (V) _____135
Jalapeño Pickled Vegetables (V) _____136
Pickled Beets with Hard-Boiled Eggs (V) _____137
Roasted Beets (V) _____138
Hard-Boiled Eggs (V) _____139
Smoked Hard-Boiled Eggs (V) _____140
Spiced Mandarin Oranges (V) _____141
Feta Cheese and Olives with Rosemary (V) _____142

Vegetables

Sautéed Vegetables (V) _____146
Cheese-Stuffed Zucchini (V) _____147
Roasted Stuffed Chayote (V) _____149
Jalapeño Scalloped Corn (V) _____151
Honey Cumin Roasted Cauliflower (V) _____153
Corn-Stuffed Roasted Tomato (V) _____155

Potatoes, Pasta, and Rice

Twice-Baked Potatoes (V) _____158
Mashed Potatoes (V) _____159
Dutch-Oven Scalloped Potatoes (V) _____160
Rosemary Roasted Red Potatoes (V) _____161
Cheese Tortellini Sautéed in EVOO (V) _____162
Pasta Primavera (V) _____163
Vegetarian Spanish Rice (V) _____165
Rice Primavera (V) _____166
Herb and Cheese Rice (V) _____168
Orange Garlic Rice (V) _____169

Beef, Fish, Chicken, Turkey, and Pork

Duo of Bacon-Wrapped Grilled
Beef Medallions with Roasted Garlic Cream Sauce _____172
Bacon-Wrapped Meatloaf with Mushroom Au Jus _____174
Swedish Meatballs _____175
Country-Fried Steak _____176

Fish or Chicken Cooked in a Paper Sack with Vegetables ___ 178
Grilled or Baked Salmon with Spiced Mandarin Oranges ___ 180
Rosemary Roasted Chicken Quarters
with Roasted Red Bell Pepper Sauce ___ 181
Cherry Chicken ___ 183
Grilled Chicken with Feta Cheese, Olives, and Rosemary ___ 184
Turkey Divan ___ 185
Roast Pork Loin with Rhubarb Sauce ___ 186
Stuffed Baked Pork Chops with Green Tomato Sauce ___ 188
Corn Bread ___ 189
Corn Bread Stuffing ___ 190
Bacon Egg Potato Pie ___ 191

Desserts

Bread Pudding (V) ___ 194
    Chocolate Caramel Sauce (V) ___ 195
Baked Pears (V) ___ 196
Spice Cake (V) ___ 197
Peach Cobbler (V) ___ 198
Pound Cake with Peaches, Pears, and
Raisins Soaked in Spiced Rum Sauce (V) ___ 199
    Spiced Rum Sauce ___ 201
S'mores Parfait (V) ___ 202
Filo Cups Filled with Strawberries and Chocolate (V) ___ 203

Acknowledgments

I want to acknowledge Kroger for the high quality of the foods I purchased there to produce the pictures in this recipe book.

Introduction

Food! What is not to love about the word? Just listen as it rolls off your tongue. F-O-O-D. What a glorious word.

> *Food: material consisting essentially of protein, carbohydrates, and fat used in the body of an organism to sustain growth, repair, vital processes, and to furnish energy. The origin of the word is Middle English* fode, *from Old English* foda, *related to Old High German* fuotar. *First use is before twelfth century.[1]*

Some other words we use to refer to food are "eats," "chow," "vittles," "feedbag," "bread," "eatables," "fare," "grub," "food-stuffs" . . . Well, you get the idea. No matter what you call it, make sure it is good. Do not be afraid to try anything.

In this recipe book, you will find recipes for appetizers, soups, vinaigrettes, salads (dinner and entree), meats, starches, and desserts. You will learn how to cook with filo dough, puff pastries, and paper lunch sacks. Some of the recipes contain ingredients found in specialty shops, such as flavor-infused vinegars, flavor-infused olive oils, and natural seed and nut oils. Cheeses (most food stores carry a large assortment of domestic and imported cheeses), filo dough, and puff pastries are available in the frozen-food section of most grocery stores. Asian and Mexican food items are available in most grocery stores, as well.

I give alternative suggestions for ingredients for most of the recipes. If you do not like nuts, then use a seed instead; if you do not like seeds but do like nuts, use them instead. Just about any food item is available gluten free, and any recipe can be made vegetarian or vegan if you know how to do that. I am not very knowledgeable on vegan cooking, although I enjoy a good vegetarian meal now and again.

---

[1] Sharon Tyler Herbst and Ron Herbst, *The Food Lover's Companion* (Hauppauge, NY: Barron's Educational Series, 2001).

All of the recipes in this book are made for two servings. In some of the recipes you will find pronunciation spellings for some of the ingredients and cooking terms with my definition of what they are. These will have an asterisk before the definition.

I have crossreferenced many recipes. I feel it is not necessary to give the directions for how to make chicken broth or how to toast nuts and seeds in every recipe they are used in. I will refer you to the first recipe in this book that uses that ingredient. The name of the recipe I am referring you to will be in **bold**. Any recipe that is vegetarian will have (V) next to the recipe name.

You will notice that some vinaigrettes I make without EVOO, because it interferes with the taste. This does not apply in every case; each vinaigrette is different, and it depends on all the ingredients.

All the measurements I give for garlic, shallots, herbs, onions, and nuts are after they have been chopped, ground, blended, or pureed. I have also included the list of cooking terms and meanings, measurements, abbreviations, equivalents, and oven temperatures.

I hope you enjoy reading, preparing, eating, and sharing with family and friends all the recipes in *All About the Love of Food* as much as I have in creating and sharing with my family and friends. Now on to the adventure. ENJOY!

But before you do, remember: Always read a recipe all the way through before starting to cook to make sure you have all the ingredients.

Cooking Terms and Meanings

- **Appetizer**: any bite-sized food served before the meal to wet and excite the palate
- **Bake**: to cook by dry heat in the oven
- **Baste**: to moisten food as it cooks with liquid such as melted fat, drippings, or fruit juice
- **Bistro**: a small café usually serving modest, down-to-earth food and wine
- **Boil**: to cook in boiling water
- **Bouquet garni**: a bunch of herbs tied together or put in cheesecloth used to flavor soups, stews, and stocks. The classic trio is parsley, thyme, and bay leaf.
- **Braised**: to cook meat by searing in fat, then simmering in covered dish in small amount of moisture
- **Brine**: to soak meats in a strong solution of water and salt. Sometimes a sweetener or herbs are added.
- **Broil**: to cook food directly under heat source
- **EVOO**: extra-virgin olive oil
- **Fresh-ground black pepper**: dried peppercorns put through a pepper grinder
- **Flambé**: to use alcohol as the burning agent causing caramelization, enhancing flavor
- **Fry**: to cook in hot fat or grease
- **Grill**: to cook directly over open charcoal or wood fire
- **Gourmet**: food that is of the highest quality, perfectly prepared and artfully presented
- **Hors d'oeuvre**: small, savory, one- or two-bite appetizers usually served with cocktails
- **Kosher salt**: a coarse-grained salt containing no additives
- **Marinate**: to soak food in a particular liquid to infuse flavors and tenderize meats
- **Parboil**: to cook in boiling water until partially done
- **Poach**: to cook by surrounding with simmering liquid (not boiling)

- **Roast**: to cook by dry heat, usually in oven
- **Sauce**: a flavored liquid used to enhance and bring out the natural flavors in food
- **Sauté**: to cook in a small quantity of hot oil in a skillet
- **Sear**: to brown the outside surface quickly by high heat
- **Simmer**: to cook in liquid slowly on top of the stove
- **Soup**: any combination of fruits, vegetables, meats, poultry, fish, or seafood cooked in a liquid, then served hot or cold
- **Steam**: to cook by steam arising from boiling liquid
- **Steam bake**: to cook in the oven in a pan submerged halfway in liquid
- **Sweating**: to cover and cook at low temperature until flavor and moisture are released
- **Vinaigrettes**: any combination of vinegars, oils, herbs, or fruits blended to use as a dressing for salads or marinades

Measurements, Abbreviations, and Equivalents

c.: Cup
tbls.: Tablespoon
tsp.: Teaspoon
oz.: Ounce
lb.: Pound
ea.: Each
pt.: Pint
qt.: Quart
gal.: Gallon
sq.: Square
doz.: Dozen
pkg.: Package
KS: Kosher salt
FGBP: Fresh-ground black pepper
dash: Less than 1/8 teaspoon
IQF: Individually quick frozen, found in the frozen section of the grocery

3 teaspoons = 1 tablespoon
16 tablespoons = 1 cup
1 cup = 1/2 pint
2 cups = 1 pint
2 pints = 4 cups = 1 quart
4 quarts (liquid) = 1 gallon
8 quarts (solid) = 1 peck
4 pecks = 1 bushel
16 ounces (dry weight) = 1 pound
4 tablespoons = 1/4 cup
5 1/3 tablespoons = 1/3 cup
8 tablespoons = 1/2 cup
10 2/3 tablespoons = 2/3 cup
12 tablespoons = 3/4 cup
14 tablespoons = 7/8 cup

Oven Temperatures

Slow: 250–300 degrees
Slow moderate: 325 degrees
Moderate: 350 degrees
Quick moderate: 375 degrees
Moderately hot: 400 degrees
Hot: 425–450 degrees
Very hot: 475–500 degrees

Appetizers

Filo-Wrapped Brie with Almonds, Raspberries, and Balsamic Drizzle (V)

1 pkg. filo dough
1 small wheel of brie cheese
1 c. melted butter
1/2 c. untoasted, sliced almonds
6 ea. red raspberries
1 ea. egg
Balsamic vinegar (any flavor)

Filo dough! What is that? Phyllo (FEE-loh) is the correct Greek spelling; the American spelling is filo. It is a pastry used in a lot of Greek cooking such as baklava and spanakopita. It is paper thin and bakes up really flaky and crisp.

Make sure the filo dough is not frozen. If it is, let thaw at least 1 hour before handling. Filo dough is very delicate and paper thin. When working with filo dough, keep the pile of dough covered with a damp (not wet) cloth. Between working with layers, it dries out very fast and gets crumbly.

French brie (BREE) is considered the best and dates back to the eighth century. This cheese is made from whole, skimmed, or partially skimmed cow's milk. The flavors range from rich, sweet, and nutty to pungent and savory. Brie has a creamy, buttery center covered with a rind that is edible.

Cut the brie cheese into 4 pieces using a knife dipped in warm water to prevent the cheese from sticking to the knife. Melt the butter; be careful not to burn. The almonds can be crushed into small pieces or left whole. The reason they are not toasted is because they may overcook and get burnt when baking with the filo and cheese.

Whip the egg with a small amount of water, using a fork to remove the membranes; they are a mess if they get on the pastry brush then onto the filo dough. On a clean, dry surface, lay 1 sheet of filo dough after carefully unrolling the stack of dough. Brush well and carefully with the melted butter. Add another sheet of filo dough, and brush well and carefully with melted butter. Do this 3 more times, making 5 layers. Use a pizza cutter or sharp knife to cut filo into 6 pieces. Set 2 aside.

In the center of the other 4, place the brie cheese on top with 3 raspberries. Brush the edges with the egg wash, then pull all 4 corners together and twist to seal. Brush outside with egg wash and place on a cookie sheet sprayed well with nonstick spray, then put in a preheated, 350-degree oven for 5 minutes. If filo isn't flaky and golden brown, leave in oven for another 3 minutes. Oven temps vary—some may take 5 minutes, some 8 or 10.

Remove from oven and let sit for 2 minutes. Carefully remove from cookie sheet to serving plates. Drizzle with balsamic vinegar; I suggest a fruit-infused flavor. With the 2 pieces of filo dough left over, brush with more melted butter, sprinkle with cinnamon sugar, and bake top with ice cream.

Another use for filo dough is to wrap around a cooked piece of meat, sealed side down, brush with melted butter or olive oil, and bake until the filo is golden brown and crispy.

Wild Mushrooms in Filo Cups (V)

1 pkg. filo dough
1/4 lb. crimini mushrooms
1/4 lb. shitake mushrooms
1/4 lb. button mushrooms
1/4 lb. gouda cheese (smoked or plain)
1 tsp. chopped garlic
KS
FGBP
Shaved parmesan cheese
1 c. melted butter
Wild mushroom EVOO
Medium-sized cupcake pan
Pan spray

Never wash mushrooms; they soak up the water. Instead, wipe them off with a damp cloth. Julienne cut (cut in strips) or dice them, stems and all. If you do not want to use the stems for this, save them for cooking in soups, sauces, baking, or omelets. There is a lot of flavor in the stems.

In a hot sauté pan, add some wild mushroom EVOO, mushrooms, salt, and pepper. Cook until tender. Turn off heat and set aside. Preheat oven to 350 degrees. Prepare filo dough in layers (the same way as in the recipe for **Filo-Wrapped Brie with Almonds, Raspberries, and Balsamic Drizzle**). Spray the cupcake pan well with pan spray. Cut the filo dough into 6 pieces with a sharp knife or pizza cutter. Gather up the corners of the filo dough and place into muffin tins that have been sprayed well with pan spray. Press against the sides, and let the top hang over the edges. Place in the oven for 5 minutes to bake. It should be golden brown and crispy. If not, leave in the oven another minute and check again. Repeat if necessary.

While the filo dough is baking, cut the gouda cheese into pieces small enough to fit in the bottom of the filo cups, or shred. The filo dough will burn easy. The pastry will be puffy; press down center and fill halfway with the gouda cheese then mushroom mixture on top with shaved parmesan cheese.

Return to oven until mushroom mixture is hot and cheese is melted. Remove from oven and let sit for 2 minutes. Carefully remove and place on serving plates, then drizzle with more wild mushroom EVOO. If you think the wild mushroom EVOO will be too much mushroom taste, try basil or garlic. Fine-diced, precooked chicken or pork can be added to this recipe.

Extra-virgin olive oil is the very first press of the olives (referred to as the "first cold press") with 1 percent acidity.

Shrimp-Filled Filo Cups with Lemongrass-Mint Balsamic and Toasted Sesame Seed Oil

1 pkg. frozen baby shrimp
1 pkg. filo dough or premade filo cups (in freezer section)
1 tsp. chopped garlic
2 tbls. chopped green onion or chives
3 tbls. lemongrass-mint balsamic
2 tbls. Japanese toasted sesame seed oil
1/4 tsp. KS
1/2 tsp. FGBP
1 lg. serving platter or 2 small appetizer plates
(Fresh mint sprigs or toasted sesame seeds are optional)

Lemongrass—also called citronella root or sereb—is a common ingredient in Thai and Vietnamese cooking. You can find it dry or fresh in Asian markets and some supermarkets. The stalk is very woody and needs to be cut into small pieces and pounded before chopping.

Shrimp (crustacean: kruh-STAY-shuhn) is one of two main varieties of shellfish; the other is mollusk (MAHL-uhsk). Shrimp is sold by count, which means 11–15 count is how many it takes to make a pound of that size. When cooked, a pound of raw shrimp will be 1/2 to 3/4 lbs. of cooked meat.

Why do I say filo dough or premade filo cups in this recipe? I want you to know you have 2 options in filo cups. If you do not want to take the time to make them from fresh dough, then buy the premade, frozen cups; they are in the frozen section along with the frozen dough. I prefer to make my own! It is fun, and they also look and taste better. In a pinch, the premade will work.

Thaw frozen baby shrimp overnight in the fridge or in running, cold water. Drain off water and place baby shrimp in a clean, dry kitchen towel. Wring out excess water, making shrimp fairly dry. The shrimp can be chopped smaller or used as is.

It is fully cooked, so no cooking is needed unless you want to serve this appetizer hot. To serve cold, mix all the ingredients together and fill the thawed filo cups. To thaw them, place on a serving platter or cookie sheet and set out at room temperature for about 10 minutes. To serve as a hot appetizer, preheat oven to 350 degrees. When the oven is hot, put the filo cups in the oven for just a few minutes to get hot. While they are heating, cook the shrimp filling, keeping an eye on the filo cups in the oven (they will burn easily).

To prepare fresh filo dough in layers, refer to the recipe for **Filo-Wrapped Brie with Almonds, Raspberries, and Balsamic Drizzle**. In a skillet on the stove that has been heated, add the toasted sesame-seed oil and garlic. Sauté until the garlic is tender. Add the shrimp, green onions or chives, and the lemongrass-mint balsamic. Stir about a minute. Spoon the shrimp filling into the hot filo cups. This can be returned to the oven for a minute or so, but no longer. Remove from oven and place on a serving plate.

A sprig of fresh mint can be added to garnish, or use toasted sesame seeds. Toasting the sesame seeds releases the oil, adding more flavor and aroma. If you are adding toasted sesame seeds, here are the directions on how to toast the sesame seeds: Heat a skillet until it is hot, adding no oil or pan spray. Add the sesame seeds and stir until they are golden brown. Be careful; they burn easily. Black sesame seeds can also be used; they toast the same way, as well as all seeds.

If there is shrimp mix left over, try adding it to the dinner salad or refrigerate to use the next day. I think this would be a great way to use leftover salmon—grilled, smoked, poached, or baked. If you like onion but not green onion or chives, then I suggest using red onion.

Stuffed Mushrooms

8 ea. lg. button mushrooms
1/4 c. onion
1/4 c. bell pepper
1/4 c. bacon
1/2 c. shredded cheese (your choice)
1/4 tsp. FGBP
1/2 tsp. garlic
Cookie sheet
Baker's rack
Pan spray

> *Fungi (FUN-guy) is Italian for mushroom.[2] No matter what language you speak, fungi is mushroom. There are about 1,000 varieties all over the world—all different sizes, shapes, and colors.* "

Mushrooms should not be put into water to wash unless you are going to use them right away. The same thing with strawberries and raspberries. This is because they soak up the water and will go bad faster. I suggest using a damp cloth to wipe them off. Preheat the oven to 350 degrees. Remove the stems, but do not throw away; you are using them as part of the stuffing. Spray the cookie sheet and baker's rack well, and place the mushrooms with stems removed open-side down on the rack placed on top of the cookie sheet. Place this in the preheated oven for 10 to 15 minutes to precook the mushrooms. This takes the shrinkage out of the mushrooms and removes the extra liquid.

Remove from oven and let sit at room temperature to cool off or place in the fridge to chill. While they are cooling off, chop all the ingredients finely, preheat a skillet, add the chopped bacon and sauté to the crispness you desire, then add all the other ingredients except the cheese. Sauté until tender.

---

[2] Ibid.

Turn the mushrooms open-side up. If there is any liquid in the center, dab with a paper towel to remove excess liquid. Leave the mushrooms on the rack to return to the oven. Mix half of the cheese with the sautéed bacon and veggies. Spoon into the mushroom caps, then top with the rest of the cheese and return to the oven for 10 minutes to melt cheese. Remove from the oven and place on appetizer plates. Serve hot.

If you are making these stuffed mushrooms for a large group, remove them from the rack after draining and put in a baking dish that has been sprayed well with pan spray to bake. The foods you can use to stuff mushrooms with are endless, such as seafoods, nuts, sausage, ground chicken, turkey, beef, herbs, chilies, and cheeses. There are other varieties of mushrooms you can use to stuff, like crimini, which is a baby portabella mushroom. Portabella mushrooms are great for stuffing. There are black gills inside where the stem is removed. Scrape out the gills with a spoon and throw them away. You can use them with the gills in, but they are much better with them removed. Morel mushrooms are also great to stuff.

Buffalo Spinach Artichoke Dip (V)

1/4 c. salad oil + 2 tbls.
1/4 c. flour
2 c. milk
FGBP to taste
1/4 c. buffalo sauce
1/2 c. cream cheese
1/2 c. Monterey Jack cheese
1 c. onion
2 tbls. garlic
4 c. fresh spinach
2 c. artichoke hearts

I start this recipe with roux, a thickener made of oil and flour or butter and flour cooked together for thickening. I give a more detailed recipe and description for roux below.

> *Roux (ROO) is a cooked blend of flour and fat (usually butter and flour) in equal amounts. White and blond roux are made with butter. Brown roux is made using pork or beef drippings. The ratio is usually equal amounts of each. Sometimes a little more flour needs to be added.*

In a skillet, heat oil. Add flour and stir well. Cook until well mixed; do not cook until brown. This is a blond; the butter is melted slowly so it doesn't burn. The flour is mixed in and cooked at least 5 minutes to remove the starch taste. I use oil for this recipe to make the roux because butter will not work for this recipe. Slowly add milk. Cook until thick, stirring constantly on low heat. Be careful not to burn! This is a basic béchamel sauce (I give the recipe for béchamel sauce in the recipe for **Cream of Chicken Noodle**). If you add swiss and parmesan cheeses to béchamel sauce, you now have Mornay sauce (the recipe for Mornay sauce is in the recipe for **Turkey Divan**). Béchamel sauce is the basic sauce used for many cream soups and sauces.

When thick, add some FGBP to taste and slowly add cheeses, stirring until melted. Remove from heat. In a blender or food processor, add the spinach, garlic, onion, and artichoke hearts. Chop, but do not puree. In a sauté pan, add 2 tbls. EVOO. When hot, add the spinach mixture and sauté until tender, then add to the cheese sauce. Stir well. Put in a baking dish and place in a preheated, 400-degree oven to bake about 8 minutes, or until top gets browned and bubbly. Serve warm with pita chips, corn chips, or crostini (recipe for crostini in the recipe for **Brie in Puff Pastry with Pecan Pesto**). Buffalo sauce can be left out for plain spinach artichoke dip.

Antipasti Display

1/4 lb. salami
1/4 lb. pepperoni
1/4 lb. Italian ham (or any type of ham you like)
2 ea. roasted bell peppers (red, green, yellow, or orange)
1 ea. can artichoke hearts
1 c. olives (black, green, Greek, or any type of olive you like)
1 c. pepperoncini
1/4 lb. provolone cheese
1/4 lb. mozzarella cheese (fresh or processed)
1 c. EVOO
1/2 c. red wine vinegar
1 tbls. garlic
FGBP to taste
1 tbls. oregano (fresh or dried)
Crostini (the recipe is in **Brie in Puff Pastry with Pecan Pesto**)

*Antipasto (ahn-tee-PAHS-toh) literally means "before the meal." It refers to an assortment of hot and cold hors d'oeuvre. Antipasti is an assortment of cured meats, cheeses, smoked fish, olives, and marinated vegetables.

I have made this display very simple, but that does not mean you cannot add any foods you choose. I chose 3 meats and 2 cheeses for this recipe. I cut the meats into different shapes. I usually cut the salami into fourths; the ham I slice and julienne cut (cut into thin strips); the pepperoni I usually serve whole; I usually slice the provolone 1/4 inch thick, then I cut in half then in half again. If I use fresh mozzarella and it is the large balls, I slice them in half then cut into slices. If they are the small balls, I leave them whole. The roasted bell peppers can be bought in the store already roasted (do not throw away the liquid the roasted bell peppers are packed in; it is full of flavor for soups and sauces. If I use canned, I save the liquid and add to the vinegar and oil for the marinade) or you can roast them in the oven.

Preheat the oven to 350 degrees. Coat the bell peppers with EVOO or canola oil and place them on a cookie sheet. Put in preheated oven, then check every 10 minutes. Turn when they start to brown. When the skin blisters, they are done. Carefully remove from oven and place in a bowl. Cover with plastic wrap or put in a paper sack. Close tightly and let them sit for at least 30 minutes. Carefully remove from the bowl or bag. The center is full of liquid and is very hot. Carefully pull them apart or let sit until ready to use—that is even safer. Pull off the skin then remove the seeds and membranes. Do not rinse in water; that removes flavor. Dice or julienne cut the bell peppers. Open the artichoke hearts and drain. If they are whole, cut into fourths. I leave the olives whole; just drain them. The pepperoncinis are used whole as garnish, or they can be cut up. Scissors work great for that, but cut them up over the bowl you're going to mix the vinegar and oil into. A large platter or divided vegetable tray will work. The vegetables can be marinated a few days ahead. Mix the EVOO and red wine vinegar with the garlic, oregano, and FGBP. The liquid from the roasted red bell peppers can be added to the mix as well. Add the bell peppers, artichoke hearts, and olives, then mix well and let sit to marinate.

To assemble the platter, alternate all the ingredients like so: meat, cheese, veggies, meat, cheese, veggies. Continue until all the ingredients are used. Garnish with the pepperoncinis, either whole or cut up. After you remove all the marinated veggies, if there is some of the vinaigrette left in the bowl, drizzle over the display. Serve with crostini or fresh-sliced Italian bread.

Grilled Fruit Kabobs (V)

2 ea. cube honeydew
2 ea. cube cantaloupe
1/4 pear
1/4 apple
2 ea. wood skewer
Apple balsamic vinegar
Tuscan herb EVOO
KS
FGBP

*Kebab or kabob (kuh-BOB): food that is cut into small
pieces, marinated, put on wood sticks, then grilled.*

*Skewer (SKYOO-uhr) is made of either wood or metal with
a ring usually at the end of the metal type. They are sharply
pointed on one end.*

If you have never grilled melons before, you are in for a
great, sweet treat! Grilling really brings out the sweetness of the
melons, and if they get a little crisp on the edges, boy, is that
great.

Peel honeydew and cantaloupe, then cut in half. Remove
seeds and throw away. Cut into large, bite-sized pieces. Cut apple
and pear into fourths, then cut each piece into 2 pieces. Place
on wood skewers (soak your wood skewers in water at least 1
hour before using; this will prevent them from catching fire) as
follows: 1 cube honeydew, 1 piece apple, 1 cube cantaloupe, 1
piece pear.

Dip in a mix of 1 part apple balsamic to 2 parts Tuscan herb
EVOO.

*Balsamic (bal-SAH-mihk) is made in the area of Modena,
Italy. It is made from white Trebbiano grapes that are cooked
and aged from 3 to 100 years in wood barrels.*

Place on grill and sprinkle with salt and pepper, turning often. They will burn easily. It should take a matter of minutes if left on grill too long for melons to turn to mush. Remove from grill. Place on serving platter or in chafer to serve.

In my recipe book *Live Well Eat Well: Janie's Twist on Salads, Sandwiches, and Wraps* on page 167 is a salad: **Janie's Fire-Roasted Fruit and Chicken**. This recipe has grilled melons and pineapple along with chicken. When I created this recipe, I had never grilled melons before, but I had eaten grilled pineapple. All I can say is bring on the grill and fruits—any fruits!

Vegetable Kabobs (V)

2 ea. lg. button mushroom
2 ea. zucchini piece
6 ea. pieces onion
2 ea. bell pepper piece
Balsamic vinegar
Tuscan herb EVOO
KS
FGBP
1 ea. wood skewer

Leave mushrooms whole. Wipe with damp cloth to remove dirt. Slice zucchini long way, cut into bite-size pieces. Peel the onion, cut into 1/2, cut each 1/2 again making 4 pieces. Cut each of these 4 pieces in the center. Separate into clusters of 3. Cut the top and bottom off the bell pepper. Cut down the side lying open. Using a paring knife, remove the membranes and seeds. Cut the pepper into bite-size pieces. Put on a skewer in this order: mushroom, zucchini, onion, then pepper. Mix the vinegar and oil together using 1 part balsamic to 2 parts EVOO. Dip kabobs in this marinade. The kabobs can marinate for several hours or overnight in the balsamic and EVOO. Then place on grill. Sprinkle with salt and pepper, turning often to prevent burning. These should take about 6 to 8 minutes to cook. Remove from grill. Place on serving platter or in chafer. Do not forget to soak the skewers in water for at least 1 hour before using. To make this an entree meal that is vegetarian, place kabobs on top of cooked brown or white rice cooked with herbs and vegetable broth, or noodles and herbs cooked in vegetable broth.

Duck and Fruit Kabobs

4 oz. marinated duck meat
1/2 ea. apple (red, green, or yellow)
1/2 ea. pear
2 ea. wood skewer
Apple balsamic vinegar
Tuscan herb EVOO
KS
FGBP

Duck? Why duck? If you do not like duck, use chicken or pork and prepare them the same way.

Soak skewer in water for 1 hour. This will prevent it from burning when placed on grill. Cut the duck breast into 1 oz. pieces, then place in a pan or bowl. Toss with the apple balsamic vinegar and Tuscan herb EVOO using 1 part balsamic to 2 parts EVOO. Cover and refrigerate for no more than 4 hours.

Remove from vinegar and oil and transfer to another bowl. Do not discard vinegar and oil; it will be used to baste kabobs during cooking. Heat a large skillet and spray generously with pan spray. Add a small amount of the Tuscan herb EVOO. Add the duck, and sauté until about halfway done. The reason for this is because the fruit will overcook and be mushy while waiting for the duck to be done. Pour into strainer or onto a paper towel to drain, and cool enough to handle. Cut the apple half into 4 pieces. Cut the pear half into 4 pieces. Remove the skewers from the water. Discard water. Place 1 piece of pear on skewer followed by 1 piece of duck then 1 piece of apple. Repeat this pattern once more.

Lay kabob on a sheet pan or in a pan, and continue building duck kabobs until desired amount is made. Generously sprinkle with black pepper and salt. These kabobs can be made up to a day ahead if you toss the apples and pear pieces after cutting in the apple balsamic to slow down browning. To cook these duck kabobs, start a charcoal fire and let the coals get white hot. Brush grill with pan spray. Lay kabobs on hot grill and brush with marinade when first on grill, then every time they are turned, turning often to prevent burning and help with even cooking. I would say they should not be on the grill more than 10 minutes. Remove from grill. Serve hot.

If serving as an appetizer, place in a warm chafer or on a serving platter. If serving as an entree, I suggest serving with duck kabobs on top of rice.

> *Wild rice is actually not a rice. It has a nutty and chewy texture. It is actually a long-grain marsh grass native to the Great Lakes area.*

Brie in Puff Pastry
with Pecan Pesto (V)

1 pkg. frozen puff pastry (thawed)
1 ea. egg
1 ea. small wheel of brie cheese
Pecan pesto (recipe follows)
Baking sheets
Cookie sheet
Pan spray
Pastry brush
Crostini (recipe follows)

> *Puff pastry: In French it is* pâte feuilletée. *It is made by placing pieces of fat, usually butter, between layers of dough, rolling it out flat, folding again, adding more butter, folding, and rolling. This is done 6 to 8 times, making hundreds of layers of dough. When baked, the butter melts, producing steam that causes the dough to puff and separate into hundreds of flaky layers.*

The rind is also, in my opinion, very tasty. I cut it up and add to some pasta dishes. They don't melt completely, but are great for adding texture and flavor. If I make a sauce with brie, I trim off the rind, as it does not melt completely. Brie is also great used in sauces and pasta dishes with other cheeses. I even like to slice it and eat with crackers or crostini.

Preheat the oven to 350 degrees. Make the pecan pesto and set aside until ready to use. It does not have to be refrigerated at this point; do so after done with it. Crack the egg and add the 1 tbls. water. Whip with a fork. On a flat surface such as a cutting board, place the sheet of puff pastry. If it is frozen, let it thaw before unfolding, as it breaks easily. Lay flat and place the round wheel of brie you have removed from the package on the puff pastry. Cut out a circle about 1 inch larger than the brie. Using a sharp slicing knife or small cheese knife dipped in hot water (this prevents the cheese from sticking badly to the knife) with the wheel of brie lying flat, slice through the center (as you would a layer cake) to make 2 layers. Remove the top half and set aside. Take another sheet of puff pastry and lay on a flat surface. Lay the top half of the wheel of brie in the center and cut the same size circle out of the puff pastry. You will use this after the next step. On top of the brie cheese laying on the puff pastry, add a nice layer of the pecan pesto. Don't worry if you do not use it all; save it for another time. Place the other half of brie on top. Pull the sides of the puff pastry up over the top. This will not completely cover the top of the cheese. Dip the pastry brush in the egg wash. Brush the sides all around the cheese and the puff pastry that is on the top. With your hands, smooth out the puff pastry. This will seal it to the cheese. Next, pick up the cheese and puff pastry and turn over. Place on top of other circle of puff pastry, then pull sides up over the top. Use the egg wash again to seal the puff pastry to the other.

If you are using pastry paper, place on the cookie sheet and spray with pan spray. Place the wheel of cheese and puff pastry in the center with the side you just sealed facing down. Brush the wheel again with egg wash, then place in the preheated, 350-degree oven to bake for 15 to 20 minutes, or until the puff pastry is golden brown and puffed up some. Decorations can be cut out of the leftover puff pastry, dipped in the egg wash, then placed on top to decorate before putting in the oven. This can be made several days ahead, placed in the freezer, removed from the freezer, and placed right in the hot oven to bake. It can also be stored for several days in the fridge uncovered; plastic will stick to the puff pastry if you cover it. It can also be baked a few days before and kept in the fridge uncovered to be served cold.

When serving from the oven, let sit outside oven for 30 minutes before cutting into. The cheese will set up some and not spread all over the serving plate. Carefully remove from cookie sheet to serving plate to cut. It is best if it is cut as it is being eaten rather than all at one time. If it is right from the oven, if cooked the day before then refrigerated, it will be set up. The balsamic can be drizzled over the hot wheel right from the oven to soak into the puff pastry, or drizzled when served. Guests can serve themselves with a cheese knife with the option of placing on a crostini, or without the extra bread, or you can slice place on crostini to serve.

No matter how you serve this, your guests will love it. The cheese can also be cut into single serving pieces then wrapped in the puff pastry for individual appetizers. Fresh berries and nuts can be used in the center along with or instead of the pecan pesto. The berries can be mashed or left whole. Also, brown sugar and nuts are great baked inside the brie.

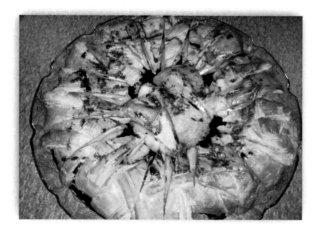

Pecan Pesto (V)

1/4 c. pecans toasted
1/4 c. shredded parmesan cheese
1/4 c. fresh basil leaves
1 tbls. fresh garlic cloves
EVOO
Food processor or blender
1 tsp. FGBP

Pesto (peh-stoh) in Italian means "pounded." Before electricity, it was made using mortar and pestle.

Pesto makes a great alternative to tomato sauces for pizza or pasta. In the food processor or blender, combine everything except the EVOO. Blend well. Add the EVOO slowly, drizzling to make a paste not too moist, not too dry. Unfortunately, there is no set amount of EVOO to add. Traditional pesto has pine nuts, not pecans. If you prefer pine nuts, by all means, use them! Toasting them increases the flavor. Toasting any nuts or seeds increases the flavor. This pesto will keep in the fridge several weeks and can be used for many recipes in place of another sauce such as tomato or alfredo.

Crostini (V)

1 ea. loaf of French or Italian bread
EVOO (plain or herb infused)
Cookie sheet

*Crostini (kroh-STEE-nee) in Italian means "little toasts."

Preheat the oven to 350 degrees. Slice the bread about 1/4 inch thick and generously coat with the EVOO. Place on cookie sheet in 350-degree oven. Let bake until toasted and golden brown. Leftover crostini are great in soups.

Soups

Italian Bean

1 ea. can cannellini beans
1/2 c. celery
1/2 c. carrots
1/2 c. onion
1 tbls. Italian seasoning
1 tbls. chopped garlic
1 ea. can diced or whole Italian tomatoes
4 c. water, chicken stock or broth, or beef stock or broth (the recipes for making stock and broth can be found on the next pages)
1/2 tsp. KS
1 tsp. FGBP
2 tbls. EVOO
2 qt. cooking pot

Soup is any combination of meats, seafood, fish, chicken, or vegetables cooked slowly in a liquid. Soups can be thick or thin, hot or cold.

I prefer my soups made chunky and hearty with lots of vegetables, garlic, herbs, and meats including beef, chicken, pork, seafood, or fish. Any soup can be made vegetarian, even though I cannot imagine a potato soup without bacon or chicken broth. Now on to making the soup!

Wash the celery. Dice into desired size, large or small (your choice). Wash, dice carrots into desired size. Peel and dice the onion. In the pot, add the EVOO over medium heat. Let get hot but not smoking; EVOO catches fire easily. Add the celery, carrots, onion, garlic, Italian seasoning, and tomatoes. Stir. Cover. Let simmer for about 10 minutes. Stir every few minutes. If starting to brown, turn heat down. After vegetables get tender, add the water, chicken stock or beef stock, salt, and pepper. Turn heat down to low. Let simmer about 30 minutes. Open the can of beans. Drain. Rinse (I rinse the canned beans because the starch in the beans makes the soup cloudy). Add to soup. Let simmer until beans get hot. Ham, salami, pepperoni, or any meat you like, including fish or seafood, can be added, as well as crushed red chilies or jalapeños. Bell peppers are also a nice addition. Chicken broth can be used instead of chicken stock.

The difference between stock and broth is there are no herbs or other seasoning used in making broth. Both of them are slow simmered and strained.

This soup or any other soup is unbelievable served in a bread bowl.

Stock

*Stocks: the results of cooking vegetables, herbs, beef, or fish in
water to bring out the flavors.*

2 c. chicken meat (white, dark, bone in, deboned, or leftover for
chicken stock), beef (scraps, bones, leftover steak, roasts cut up,
you get the idea), fish (pieces or scraps), seafood (including shells
from shrimp or lobster, shrimp pieces, lobster pieces, clams,
oysters), pork (scraps, bones, leftover)
1 c. celery
1 c. onion
1 c. carrots
4 c. water
1 tsp. KS
1 1/2 tsp. FGBP
1 tbls. garlic
1/4 c. herbs (basil, oregano, thyme, parsley, Italian seasoning, bay
leaf)

The combination of carrots, onions, celery, and herbs used
together to make a stock is called mirepoix.

*Mirepoix (mihr-PWAH): This combination is also used
to layer the bottom of a roasting pan then placing raw meat,
chicken, fish, seafood, or pork on top to roast.*

This combination of vegetables and herbs can be used to roast
bones to make a rich, dark stock. Add tomato paste on top to
enhance the color and flavor of the stock, and a handful of garlic
cloves can be added or chopped garlic. I like to add garlic to all
my stocks. Roast the vegetables about 30 minutes. When you
remove the pan from the oven, use wine or water to deglaze the
pan you roast in. To do this, pour about 1 c. in the pan. Use a
metal spoon or spatula to scrape the pan to loosen all that great
stuff stuck to the bottom of the pan. Dump it into the pot you
are going to cook the stock in. Now back to making a pot of

stock: Use a large pot. Add the water, mirepoix, chicken, beef, fish, seafood, or pork, and herbs, garlic is optional, salt, and pepper. Let come to a boil. Turn down heat. Simmer for at least 1 hour; 4–6 is even better. The longer it is simmered, the richer the flavor. The longer you cook the stock to do what is called a reduction, the richer the flavor is. If a foam forms on top it can be removed with a spoon. I use my kitchen strainer to strain the stock.

To make vegetable stock, use any combination of vegetables you like. I do not use potatoes, it makes the stock starchy; nor broccoli or cauliflower, they tend to take over the flavor. Here are some vegetables I suggest: carrots, celery, onion (any variety), zucchini, yellow squash, turnips. Herbs I suggest are basil, oregano, rosemary, sage, thyme, or Italian seasoning. I always add plenty of garlic cloves or chopped garlic, KS, and FGBP. Of course, you can use whole peppercorns. Put everything in a large stock pot. Cover with water. Let come to a boil. Turn heat down. Let simmer for several hours, then strain. I do not peel any of the vegetables, but I do cut the stems off of all of them. Tomatoes can also be added for flavor. The color will have a pink tinge from the tomatoes.

Broth

Broth: the result of slowly cooking water, chicken, beef, or fish.

4 c. water
2 c. raw chicken meat (white, dark, bone in, deboned, or leftover for chicken stock), beef (scraps, bones, leftover steak, roasts cut up, you get the idea), fish (pieces or scraps), seafood (including shells from shrimp or lobster, shrimp pieces, lobster pieces, clams, oysters), pork (scraps, bones, leftover)
1 tsp. KS
1/2 tbls. FGBP

The difference between a stock and a broth is that the broth is *not* made with vegetables, garlic, or herbs. It is nothing but water, salt, and pepper with the chicken, beef, fish, seafood, or pork. Leave the fat on the meat for a better broth. Let come to a boil then turn down. Simmer at least an hour; 4–6 hours is best. The longer you simmer the broth, the richer the taste is. The broth can be cooked down slowly to make a reduction that produces a richer flavor. For a really great broth, leave the fat on the meat when making the broth for more flavor. If scum collects on the top, remove with a slotted spoon or small strainer. If you put the broth in the fridge overnight, the fat will come to the surface. You can remove it for use in other dishes. Chicken fat can be used for matzo ball soup or for flavoring other foods.

Hearty Tomato (V)

1 ea. 14 oz. can tomato sauce
1 ea. 6 oz. can tomato paste
4 c. tomato juice
1/2 c. carrots
1/2 c. celery
1/2 c. onion
1 ea. 10 oz. can diced tomatoes (with or without green chilies)
1 tbls. chopped garlic
1 tbls. dried or fresh basil
1 tsp. KS
1 tsp. FGBP
2 tbls. EVOO

*Tomato paste is available in both cans and tubes. It is the end
result of cooking tomatoes down to a thick, rich, deep-red paste.*

Who does not love a good tomato soup? This recipe is for a
thick, rich, and—as the name of this recipe says—hearty soup. Peel,
dice carrots, celery, and onions in a 2 qt. stock pot. Add EVOO.
Let get hot but not to smoking point. Add vegetables, garlic, and
basil. Stir. Cover. Let simmer on low heat for about 10 minutes until
vegetables are tender. If starting to brown, turn heat down more.
When they are tender, add tomato paste, mixing in well. Let simmer
for 5 minutes, stirring often, then add tomato juice, tomato sauce,
diced tomatoes, salt, and pepper. Stir well. Let simmer 30 minutes.

If you want it creamy, add 1 c. heavy cream or milk. Sometimes
heavy cream will do what is called "breaking." This is where the
soup looks like it curdled.

There are several cheeses that would be great added to this
soup, such as brie, parmesan, or cheddar. I also love to add herbed
parmesan croutons to this soup. To make them, use a crusty,
unsliced bread, such as French or Italian. Slice the thickness you
would like, then dice. Put in a mixing bowl. Add EVOO, garlic
powder, onion powder, parmesan cheese, and Italian seasoning.
Toss well. Place on a cookie sheet. Put in 350-degree, preheated
oven until golden crispy. A pasta can be added to this soup, or rice.
I have also used this soup with pasta to make a baked pasta dish.

Spinach (Florentine) Chicken

2 c. diced chicken meat (white or dark)
4 c. chicken broth (the recipe for making chicken broth or stock
is after the recipe for **Italian Bean** soup)
2 c. spinach leaves (fresh or frozen)
1/2 c. celery
1/2 c. carrot
1/2 c. onion
1 c. mushrooms (optional)
2 tbls. chopped garlic
2 tbls. EVOO
1 tsp. oregano (fresh or dried)
1 tsp. KS
2 tsp. FGBP

*Spinach (SPIHN-ihch) originated in the Middle East and
was grown in Spain during the eighth century. That is how
it came to America. It is rich in iron and vitamins A and C.*

I have found that spinach is one of those foods that people either
love or hate. I love it raw or cooked. Some people only like it raw;
some people like it only cooked. In a pot, add the EVOO. Let get
hot, but not smoking. Add the vegetables (except spinach), chicken,
garlic, and oregano. Cover and let simmer on low for 10 minutes,
or until vegetables are tender. Stir occasionally. Be careful it does
not burn. Add broth. Turn heat to medium. Let simmer 20 minutes
or more. Add spinach. Let cook another 10 minutes. If you do
not like spinach but like kale, then use kale instead. Or, if you like
them both, use them both. Collard greens or turnip greens can also
be used, as well as cabbage. Turkey, beef, pork, seafood, or fish
would also be great in this soup. The herb you use can be changed
according to what you are replacing the chicken with. Maybe sage
for the turkey, rosemary for the beef, cilantro for the pork, and
dill for seafood or fish, or use the oregano for any of them.

Cream of Chicken Noodle

6 c. chicken broth or stock
2 c. chicken meat (white, dark, or both)
1/2 c. celery
1/2 c. carrots
1/2 c. onion
3/4 c. butter
1/2 c. flour
2 c. heavy cream, half-and-half, or whole milk (skim will not work; this is used to make the béchamel sauce)
2 c. béchamel sauce
1 tbls. garlic
2 tsp. thyme (fresh or dried)
8 oz. uncooked noodles
1 tsp. KS
2 tsp. FGBP

> *Thyme (TIME) is a member of the mint family. There are several varieties. It is native to southern Europe and the Mediterranean. Garden thyme is the most common variety used in the US. It has a somewhat minty flavor with tones of lemon. It grows on a bush with gray-green color.*

This soup is made in three stages: first stage is making the chicken broth, the second stage is making the chicken noodle soup, the third stage is making the béchamel sauce used to make the cream of chicken noodle soup. I have listed all the ingredients and quantities for this soup in one ingredient list; they are not listed in order of usage.

Chicken Broth

The recipe for making chicken broth is after the recipe for **Italian Bean** *soup.*

Roux (this roux is made with butter, unlike the recipe in **Buffalo Spinach Artichoke Dip**)
1/2 c. unsalted butter
1/2 c. flour

Heat a skillet over medium heat. Add butter or fat. Let melt but not burn. Add flour. Stir constantly with a wooden spoon until incorporated and cooked until dry, stirring constantly so it does not burn. For a white roux, cook about 3–5 minutes. For an amber or dark roux, cook until the color desired. As the roux cooks, it takes on the aroma of nuts. The longer it is cooked, the stronger the smell.

Béchamel Sauce (V)

2 c. heavy cream, half-and-half, or whole or 2 percent milk
(heavy cream gives you the best flavor, skim will not work)
1/4 c. roux (recipe on previous page)
KS and FGBP to taste
1 ea. can pan spray

In a saucepan sprayed well with pan spray, add milk product. Let simmer on low to medium heat until hot. Add roux. Whisk with a wire whip. Add salt and pepper. Continue stirring with whisk until hot and comes to a low boil and the desired thickness you want. If not thick enough, add more roux 1 tsp. at a time, mixing well. Let return to a low boil until thick.

> *Béchamel sauce is your basic white sauce. From there, other sauces that you want milk or cream based can be made as well as soups.*

Asian Chicken

4 c. chicken meat
4 c. chicken stock or broth
1 tbls. sesame oil
2 tsp. soy sauce
1 tbls. ginger (fresh or dried)
1 tbls. garlic
1 c. water chestnuts
1 c. snow peas
1 c. onions
1 c. bean sprouts
1/2 c. red bell peppers
1 c. carrots
2 tsp. KS
1 tbls. FGBP
1 tsp. crushed red peppers

Another chicken soup? What's not to love about chicken soups? The basic recipe of most chicken soups can be used to make pork or fish soups. The vegetables in this soup are prepared with different cuts. The water chestnuts come in a can, whole or sliced. I slice them if I buy them whole, or they can be chopped up smaller or cut in halves or fourths. Chop the garlic finely. Remove the strings from the snow peas. Cut in half on the bias. The onions I like to julienne cut, the bell peppers are fine diced, the carrots I like to julienne cut, the chicken I dice.

> *Julienne (joo-lee-EHN, zhoo-LYEHN): foods that are cut into a strip about the size of a matchstick.*

This is a great way to use leftover chicken or precooked, diced, frozen chicken. In a soup pot, add the sesame oil to heat on medium heat. If using raw chicken, add that to the pot with the sesame oil, then add the water chestnuts, garlic, snow peas, onions, bell peppers, and carrots. Let sauté until tender and chicken is done. The ginger can be added at this time also. When veggies are done add chicken stock, soy sauce, salt, and pepper. The crushed red chilies can be added at this time. Let simmer for at least 1 hour. Cabbage, finely sliced, can also be added, as well as mushrooms.

Chicken Enchilada

4 c. chicken meat (white or dark or both)
4 c. water, chicken stock, or broth
1 c. corn
1 c. onion (white, yellow, or red)
1 c. mild green chilies
1 tbls. garlic
2 tsp. ground cumin
2 c. diced corn tortillas
1–2 c. enchilada sauce (red or green)
2 tsp. KS
1 tbls. FGBP

This is one of those soups that you want to start with raw chicken meat. In a stock pot, add the water or chicken broth, chicken meat (on the bone or deboned, diced or whole), green chilies, garlic, peeled and diced onion, enchilada sauce, KS, and FGBP. Let come to a boil. Turn down to a simmer. Let cook for about 1 hour. This soup can also be made in a slow cooker, cooked all day or overnight. When the meat is well done, add corn and diced corn tortillas. Taste for seasonings. Add more enchilada sauce, KS, or FGBP as needed.

The reason you want to use raw chicken is because you want it cooked very well, almost shredded. If you plan on using already-cooked chicken, chop or shred it up well. Also, use chicken broth or stock instead of water. This is probably the easiest soup I have ever made. I have made this soup with both red and green enchilada sauce. I can easily say I love both ways. I suggest serving this in bowls garnished with sour cream and shredded cheddar cheese. Other ingredients you can add are fresh cilantro, jalapeños, or habañeros.

Black Bean

2 ea. 15 oz. cans cooked black beans
1 c. bacon
1/2 c. celery
1/2 c. carrots
1/2 c. onion
4 c. chicken stock or beef stock or broth, depending on the flavor
you want
1 tbls. garlic
1 tbls. ground cumin
1 tsp. FGBP
1/2 tsp. KS
Sour cream (to garnish)
Shredded cheddar cheese (to garnish)

Who does not like a good bean soup? If you do not like
black beans, you can use kidney, pinto, or butter beans, just to
mention a few.

*Black beans (turtle beans) are common dishes made in
South American countries and southern USA.*

To make this soup, dice the bacon (if you do not like bacon,
use sausage or ham instead), celery (leaves included), carrots,
onions. Chop garlic. Put a soup pot on the stove. Turn heat to
medium. Let get hot, but don't let smoke. Add the bacon, garlic,
celery, onions, carrots. Stir well and let simmer until bacon is cooked
(but not crisp) and veggies are tender. Add the cumin, salt, and
pepper.

*Cumin (UH-mihn, KYOO-mihn, KOO-mihn) is also
sometimes called cumino. It is the dried fruit of a plant in the
parsley family. It is available in amber, the most commonly
used in the US, or white and black, used more commonly
in the Middle East and Asia.*

Pour in the stock. Let come to a boil. Reduce heat. Drain and rinse the beans (this is because the starch in the beans will make the soup cloudy). Add to pot. Stir well. Taste for seasoning. Add more cumin, salt, and pepper. Let simmer until ready to serve. To serve, place in soup bowls. Sprinkle with the shredded cheese and add a dollop of sour cream. This soup, as all bean soups, can be made from dry beans. Canned beans are packed by weight. I would suggest for black beans 3 c. dry. Put them into a container, cover with cold water, and let sit overnight. They will reconstitute and double in size. Drain. Add to soup pot when the broth is hot. Let cook for about 4 hours until the beans are done.

Turkey Vegetable

1 lb. turkey meat or 4 c. cooked (white or dark)
4 c. turkey stock or broth
1/2 c. carrots
1/2 c. celery
1/2 c. onion
1/2 c. bell peppers
1/2 c. mushrooms
1/2 c. green beans (fresh, canned, or frozen)
1/2 c. corn (fresh, canned, or frozen)
1 c. potatoes
1 ea. 15 oz. can diced tomatoes
2 tsp. garlic
1 tsp. KS
2 tsp. FGBP
1 tbls. ground sage
2 c. leftover stuffing (optional)
1/2 c. oil

Turkey vegetable soup? What a great way to use up leftover turkey! If you have some stuffing left over, you might want to add 2 c. of that to the soup; it adds a lot of flavor. If you are starting this soup with raw turkey, make sure you rinse the turkey then dice into bite-sized pieces. Put in a bowl. Peel and dice carrots, dice celery (leaves included), peel and dice onion, dice bell peppers, and slice or dice mushrooms. The potatoes can be peeled or not. Dice them and set aside. Chop the garlic. Put the oil into the soup pot. Let it get hot. Add turkey, carrots, celery, onions, mushrooms, garlic, salt, pepper, and sage (do not add potatoes at this time). Sauté until the turkey is done and the vegetables are soft. Add the turkey stock (if you do not have turkey stock or broth, use chicken stock or broth). If you are using cooked turkey, add it now with potatoes, green beans, corn, and diced tomatoes (drained or not). Let come to a boil, then simmer until potatoes are done. Adjust the seasonings; add more if it is required.

Soups like this are a great way to use up leftover potatoes and turkey. This soup should be very thick and full of flavor. Here is another suggestion: add 1–2 c. turkey gravy for a richer broth.

Hearty Beef and Tomato

1 lb. raw beef or 4 c. leftover cooked beef
2 c. beef stock or broth
1 ea. 15 oz. can tomato sauce
2 c. tomato juice
1/2 c. carrots
1/2 c. celery
1/2 c. onion
1 ea. 15 oz. can diced tomatoes (with or without green chilies)
1 tbls. chopped garlic
1 tbls. dried or fresh basil
2 tsp. FGBP
2 tsp. KS
1/4 c. EVOO

This is another dish that is great made with leftover beef.

Basil (bay-zihl, ba-zihl): The ancient Greeks referred to basil as the "royal herb."

If you are making the soup from raw beef, add the beef with the vegetables to sauté, then add stock or broth. Peel and dice carrots, dice celery, chop garlic, and dice onions. In a soup pot, add EVOO. Let get hot, but not to smoking point. Add vegetables, garlic, and basil. Stir. Cover. Let simmer on low heat for about 10 minutes until vegetables are tender. If starting to brown, turn heat down more. When they are tender, add beef, tomato juice, tomato sauce, beef stock or broth, diced tomatoes, salt, and pepper. Stir well. Let simmer 30 minutes. If you are using roast beef you previously cooked and have gravy or juice from that, add it to the soup. Also, any of the vegetables you had left can be added.

Vinaigrettes

I use either a handheld blender, often called an immersion blender, food processor, or kitchen blender, to mix the vinaigrettes. As I wrote in my introduction, you will notice that some vinaigrettes I make without EVOO because it interferes with the fruit taste. This does not apply in every case. Each vinaigrette is different; it depends on all the ingredients. Some of the vinaigrettes I use xanthan gum to thicken; some do not need it.

> *Xanthan gum is made from the fermentation of corn syrup. It adds no flavor or color, just thickens dairy products, ketchup, salad dressings, and a lot of other commercially prepared foods.*

I find most vinaigrettes made with jams, jellies, or canned fruit do not need xanthan because of the natural pectin in the fruits. If you like the texture of the vinaigrette, then it is not necessary to add it. Start with 1/8–1/4 tsp. Add 1/8 tsp. Blend. Check texture; add more if needed. If you wash the berries, let them dry completely before using. I have never had a problem with berries as far as dirt on the blueberries, blackberries, or raspberries. I check the strawberries, and if they need washing I wipe them with a damp cloth. If you find you have small amounts of several vinaigrettes in the fridge, try mixing 2 or 3 together for a completely new flavor. There are 32 different vinaigrettes in this book with 18 salads. Do not be afraid to use a different vinaigrette than I suggest.

Grape Bacon

2 c. grape jelly
3/4 c. bacon grease
1 ea. slice cooked bacon
1/4 c. salad oil
1 c. rice wine vinegar
1/2 tsp. FGBP

Grape and bacon! Oh yeah!

Grapes are actually a berry that come in two color categories: white and black. The white range in colors from pale yellow-green to light green. The black range from light red to purplish black. They also come seedless or with seeds and are classified in three groups to be used for wines, table use, or commercial foods.

Bacon with anything only makes it better. I feel I have come up with the right combination. Never throw out your bacon grease; put it in a container in the fridge. Use to make popcorn, add to sautéed vegetables, or make vinaigrettes. When you cook bacon for a meal and have leftovers, put it in a ziplock bag in the freezer for when you want to add cooked bacon to a recipe. In fact, when you are cooking bacon, try making some extra to freeze for just that reason. I made this vinaigrette using fresh grapes the first time I made it. Bad idea—the skins of the grapes are bitter. I use grape jelly because all the hard work is done and the sweetness is perfect. In fact, jams and jellies make great vinaigrettes. The only exception is strawberry jam; the texture of the cooked strawberries makes the vinaigrette look like . . . well, let's just say slime. To make this vinaigrette, just put all the ingredients together and blend well. I blend all my vinaigrettes with a stick blender or immersion blender.

Roasted Red Bell Pepper El Pato (V)

1 ea. can El Pato sauce
2 c. roasted red bell pepper (canned or fresh roasted) (the directions to roast your own bell peppers is in the recipe for **Antipasti Display**)
1 tbls. garlic
1 c. cider vinegar
2 c. salad oil
1/2 tbls. oregano (dried or fresh)
1 tsp. KS
1 tsp. FGBP
1/8–1/4 tsp. xanthan gum

El Pato sauce? *I know that name* . . . Yes you do! It is the name of this wonderful Mexican chili sauce found in food stores with the Mexican food. It is a small can either red, yellow, or green. Both are delicious. I also have a recipe in my recipe book *Live Well Eat Well: Janie's Twist on Salads, Sandwiches, and Wraps*: **El Pato Vinaigrette**. If you are not sure if this recipe will be too hot for your use, add 1/2 can El Pato sauce and the rest of the ingredients using the quantities I have listed. Blend well. Taste and add more if needed. Once you open your first can of El Pato sauce, you will not stop finding uses for it. Once you make and use this vinaigrette, you will also have fun finding new dishes to use it on: marinades, add some brown sugar and you have a great BBQ sauce, put on potato salad or macaroni salad. The flavor of this vinaigrette gets better over time. Keep the leftovers in a covered container in the fridge.

Fat-Free and/or
Sugar-Free Mixed Berry (V)

1/2 c. raspberries (fresh or frozen)
1/2 c. strawberries (fresh or frozen)
1/2 c. blueberries (fresh or frozen)
1/2 c. blackberries (fresh or frozen)
1/2–1 c. sugar or artificial sweetener
1 c. raspberry vinegar or rice wine vinegar
2 c. apple juice or berry juice (no water)
1/2 tsp. KS
1/2 tsp. FGBP
1/8–1/4 tsp. xanthan gum

This is one fat-free recipe that you will not miss the oil in. Replacing the oils with fruit juice instead of water ensures a refreshing fruit flavor. Xanthan gum is definitely needed in this fruit vinaigrette because of no oil being used. Start with half the sugar blend, then taste. To make this recipe almost totally sugar free, use no-sugar-added apple or fruit juice. No sugar added means it contains only the natural sugar in the fruit. Place all the berries in a food processor, blender, or container to use a handheld blender. Add the rest of the ingredients using only half the sugar or artificial sweetener. Blend well. Taste and adjust the sweetness. If you do not like some of the berries used in this recipe, leave them out and add extra of what you do like. As with all fruit vinaigrettes, a little spice such as jalapeños, habañeros, or cayenne pepper only makes it better. Store in a closed container in the fridge. It will keep for months.

Apple Maple Cayenne Pepper (V)

1 c. apple pie filling
1/2 c. sugar or artificial sweetener
1 tbls. cinnamon
2 tsp. cayenne pepper
2 tbls. maple syrup
1/2 tsp. KS
1 tsp. FGBP
1 1/2 c. apple cider vinegar
1 1/2 c. salad oil
1/8–1/4 tsp. xanthan gum

Maple syrup is the result of tapping maple trees for the sap that is boiled down to make maple syrup. The American Indians taught the colonists how to tap the trees and boil down the sap to make what they called "sweetwater."

This tastes like apple pie with a kick: sweet and spicy with a good apple taste, hint of maple, and kick of cayenne pepper. Put all the ingredients together. Blend well. Do not overdo with the maple syrup; a hint of maple is all that is needed. If you do not like maple, then add caramel or leave it out altogether.

Bacon Avocado

1 1/2 c. bacon grease
2 ea. avocado
1 tbls. garlic
2 tbls. lemon juice
1 tsp. KS
1 tsp. FGBP
1 1/2 c. apple cider vinegar
1 1/2 c. salad oil

Avocado (a-voh-KAH-doh) is actually a fruit but is used as a vegetable. They have a nutty, buttery taste and are rich in vitamin C, thiamine, and riboflavin.

Never throw away your bacon grease. Keep a container in your fridge to add to every time you cook bacon, unless you use it right then to cook with. Try popping popcorn in it or use for mac and cheese instead of with butter. To make this great vinaigrette, combine everything together and blend well. You will notice it is rather thick; that is because of the bacon grease. When you toss it with something, it becomes creamy and melts. There are a lot of uses for this vinaigrette other than for salad. Try on a burger or sub sandwich. This is another great vinaigrette that some heat can be added to, such as crushed red chilies or jalapeños.

Tomato Mint (V)

2 1/2 c. tomatoes (canned or fresh peeled)
1/2 c. fresh mint leaves
1 tsp. KS
1 1/2 tsp. FGBP
1/2–1 c. sugar or artificial sweetener (I usually recommend starting out
with 1/2 the sweetener to start)
1 c. rice wine vinegar
1 c. salad oil
1 c. EVOO
1/8–1/4 tsp. xanthan gum

> *Mint: Since the time of the Greek era, mint has long been a
> sign of hospitality. There are over thirty varieties, with
> peppermint and spearmint being the most popular.*

If you use canned tomatoes, drain well. Save the juice for
soups or sauces. If you use fresh tomatoes, you need to blanch
them to remove skins. To do this, use a pot big enough to boil
enough water to completely submerge the tomatoes to blanch.
Use a paring knife or Tomato Shark to remove the core from
the stem end of the tomatoes. In the other end, cut through the
skin, only making an X. Drop in the boiling water. It will take
no more than 3 minutes for the skin at the core end and other
end to pull away from the meat. Remove from the pot. Put in
ice water to stop cooking and chill tomatoes. Remove them from
the ice water, peel off the skin, and cut the tomatoes in half.
Remove the seeds. Now they are ready to be blended. Combine all
ingredients. Blend well. This vinaigrette is very sweet and has a
strong mint taste.

Rhubarb (V)

2 c. rhubarb sauce (recipe follows)
1 c. apple cider vinegar
2 c. salad oil
1 tsp. dried thyme
KS
FGBP
1/2 c. sugar (if needed)
1/8–1/4 tsp. xanthan gum

Rhubarb (ROO-bahrb) is actually a vegetable, but we use it like a fruit. The stalks are the only part we can eat. The leaves contain oxalic acid and can be toxic. Rhubarb is a member of the buckwheat family. It contains a large amount of vitamin A.

Because of its extreme tartness, large quantities of sugar are added. I tried to make this vinaigrette with fresh, uncooked rhubarb, but it did not work out. The texture was grainy tasting, like I had sand in my mouth. The first step in making this vinaigrette is to make the rhubarb sauce. The recipe for **Rhubarb Sauce** can be found in the **Sauces and Au Jus** section.

Strawberry Chipotle (V)

2 tsp. garlic
3 ea. chipotle chilies
3 tsp. adobo sauce
1 c. red onion
4 c. strawberries (fresh or IQF)
1 c. cider vinegar
1 c. EVOO
1 c. salad oil
1 tsp. KS
1 tsp. FGBP
1/2–1 c. sugar
1/8–1/4 tsp. xanthan gum

> **Chipotle chili: This delicious, spicy, smoky-flavored chili is actually a smoked, dried jalapeño that is packed in cans in adobo sauce.*
>
> **Adobo sauce is a dark-red sauce made from ground chilies, herbs, and vinegar. It is used as a marinade and in many Latin dishes.*

Cut the stems off the strawberries. They can be left whole or cut up. Strawberries can be used. Open the can of chipotle chilies. Remove 3. Place with the strawberries. Add 3 tsp. of the adobo sauce, more if you like more heat. Actually the whole can of chipotle chilies with the adobo sauce can be used for extra flavor. Peel the red onion. Cut into pieces small enough to blend. Add the onion and the rest of the ingredients (I suggest you start with 1/2 c. sugar blend, taste, and add more if desired). Blend well and enjoy.

Just remember—the more chipotle chilies you add, the less strawberry you will taste, so if you want a real punch with a lot of strawberry taste, I suggest for each additional chipotle you add use 4–6 more strawberries. Do not increase anything else because the recipe will grow and be out of control. If more sugar is needed for your taste, add 1 tbls. at a time. Sweet fruit and spicy can't be beat.

Fat-Free Dried Fruit (V)

2 c. dried fruit
2 c. rice wine vinegar
4 c. apple juice or other juice
1 tbls. thyme (fresh or dried)
1/8–1/4 tsp. xanthan gum

*Dried fruit: fruit that has had all but 15–25 percent of the moisture removed.

I do not add any sugar or sweetener to this recipe; there is plenty in the dried fruit already. For some reason, the fruit is soaked in a sweetener of some sort before being commercially dried. To dry your own, use a food dehydrator or your oven. The commercial dehydrator comes with instructions that are easy to follow. You can also dry them outside, but beware of bugs and pets. Dry in the oven on 250 degrees overnight. Use baker's racks on cookie sheets. If you use strawberries, cut off the stem, lay them out on the baker's racks, and put in the preheated oven overnight (longer if needed). Some fruits take several days, like pineapple.

To make the vinaigrette, warm the vinegar either in the microwave, of which I am not a fan of using, or heat in a pot on the stove—not to boiling, just warm. Put the fruit in it and let sit until room temperature. Add the rest of the ingredients except for the xanthan gum (this is because some dried-fruit vinaigrettes are thick without adding it), then blend well. The reason I soak the dried fruit is because it is very hard to blend. If it is softened, it blends really easily.

Mirin Red Onion (V)

1 tbls. garlic
1 c. rice wine vinegar
1 c. mirin
2 c. salad oil
1 c. EVOO
1 c. red onion
1 tsp. KS
1 tsp. FGBP
1/8–1/4 tsp. xanthan gum

> *Mirin (MIHR-ihn): a rice wine that is low in alcohol that is sweet and used in a lot of Japanese cooking and available in all Asian markets.*

If you cannot find mirin—which would surprise me if you couldn't—then use sake. Peel the garlic and onion. I cut the onion into pieces so it can be blended easily. Put everything together. Blend well. This vinaigrette is especially good with a salad containing chicken, seafood, or pork. It is also a great marinade for chicken, seafood, or pork.

Smoked or Roasted Red Onion Red Bell Pepper (V)

1 c. red onion (smoked or roasted)
1/4 c. garlic (smoked or roasted)
1 c. red bell peppers (smoked or roasted)
1 c. cider vinegar
2 c. salad oil
1 tbls. rosemary (smoked or roasted)
2 tbls. sugar
1 tsp. KS
1 1/2 tsp. FGBP
1/8–1/4 tsp. xanthan gum

Smoking: There are two ways to smoke foods, cold smoking or hot smoking. Cold smoking is done with a much lower temperature of 70 degrees to 90 degrees, usually for 1–3 days instead of 4–12 hours. Hot smoking is done with temperatures of 120 degrees to 180 degrees, depending on the size of what is being smoked and how long you want to smoke.

Peel the red onion. Place in smoker for at least 60 minutes. Place the garlic in the smoker for at least 20 minutes, the red bell peppers in the smoker for at least 30 minutes. To smoke on the stove top, use wood chips soaked in water for at least 1 hour. This will prevent them from starting fire. If you have a cast-iron skillet, they work great. If not, use a cake pan with a baker's rack. Place the wood chips in the bottom and spread out. Place the rack over the top. Light the wood chips on fire. When they start to smoke, add the onions, garlic, and peppers. Cover with foil. Let cook for desired time. I suggest if you do this method you do the onions and garlic first. Remove them and add peppers. If more wood is needed, carefully remove the rack, add more wood, then replace the rack. Add peppers, cover, and let smoke. Add the fresh rosemary for the last 10 minutes of cooking.

If you use a grill outside, start either a wood or charcoal fire, let burn down, then add soaked wood chips. Place onion and garlic in a pan then place on grill along with peppers. Remove garlic and onions when done and peppers when they are done. You will need to check peppers every 10 minutes and turn.

If roasting, place the onions and garlic on a baking sheet after tossing them in salad oil. Place in 350-degree oven for no more than 10–15 minutes. Coat the bell peppers with oil, place in oven, roast for 10 minutes and turn, and check every 10 minutes, turning until skin is blistery and dark. Do not burn. Let the onions and garlic cool. Place the bell peppers in a bowl. Cover with plastic or foil for at least 1 hour. Do not uncover; steam will loosen the skin. Carefully peel the skin off the bell peppers. Be careful— the center is liquid and very hot! It will burn you. Do not rinse any of these foods off in water or any other liquid that will remove the flavor. Blend everything together and enjoy finding uses for this vinaigrette. This is a great vinaigrette for tossing with cheese tortellini and chicken.

Red Onion Strawberry (V)

3 c. strawberries fresh or IQF
1 c. red onion
1 c. rice wine vinegar
1 c. EVOO
1 c. salad oil
1/4–1/2 c. sugar or artificial sweetener
2 tsp. tarragon (fresh or dried)
1 tsp. KS
2 tsp. FGBP
1/8–1/4 tsp. xanthan gum

Tarragon (TEHR-uh-gon, TEHR-uh-guhn) is a very aromatic herb known for its anise-like flavor. It is very common is French cooking. The leaves are narrow, pointed, and dark green. Fruits pair very well with this herb as well as chicken, pork, and fish.

Never wash strawberries in water. They are like mushrooms; they soak up the water and go bad faster. If they have dirt on them, use a wet cloth to wipe them off. To make this vinaigrette, simply cut off the stems of the strawberries, peel and dice the onion.

If you use fresh tarragon, remove from the stems. If you have fresh and want to dry it, simply put in a 350-degree oven for 5 minutes or dry slowly overnight in the oven on foil or cookie sheet using only the heat from the pilot light. Fresh tarragon blends very well. The only fresh herb I have found that doesn't blend fresh is rosemary; it must be dried, as it doesn't completely blend. It is like sand.

Place all the ingredients in a food processor or blender using half the sugar (or substitute) and half the xanthan gum. Blend well.

Put everything together. Blend well.

Tomato Roasted Garlic Chive (V)

3 c. canned diced tomatoes or fresh tomatoes
1/2 c. dried chives
1/2 c. roast garlic
2 c. cider vinegar
4 c. salad oil
1 tbls. sugar or sugar substitute
1 tsp. KS
1 1/2 tsp. FGBP
1/4 tsp. xanthan gum

If using canned tomatoes, drain well. Save the liquid for vinaigrettes (the tomato juice can be used to make a fat-free vinaigrette in place of the oil), soups, or sauces. The directions for blanching fresh tomatoes to peel for recipes is in the recipe for **Tomato Mint** salad. After you have blanched and peeled the tomatoes, cut them in half, remove the seeds, then dice into 1/4- to 1/2-inch pieces. The directions for roasting garlic cloves is in the recipe for **Smoked or Roasted Red Onion Red Bell Pepper**. If you have whole bulbs, cut them in half, spray an oven-safe baking dish, add a small amount of oil, put bulbs cut-side down, and roast for 10 minutes. Check for doneness by squeezing the bulbs; they should be soft. Remove from oven, let cool, then squeeze the bulbs to release the garlic cloves. Let cool. Slice very thin. I use dried chives instead of fresh. The fresh turn brown and make the vinaigrette look bad after about 2–3 months.

> *Chives and their edible, lavender flowers are both very tasty with a mild onion flavor. They are considered an herb and are long, dark-green, hollow stems.*

The vinaigrette is not bad and does not need to be tossed out. Chives can be bought dried or you can dry your own. To dry your own, I suggest you cut them first into about 1/4-inch pieces (scissors work great for this), put on a cookie sheet or in a baking dish, then put in a 350-degree oven for 5 minutes.

Add everything together; mix by hand. Do not blend with hand blender, food processor, or blender. You will have great-tasting tomato juice.

Fat-Free Canned Fruit (V)

1 ea. can fruit (regular or no sugar added)
Juice from canned fruit
2 c. fruit juice (any flavor)
2 c. rice wine vinegar
1/2 tsp. KS
1 tsp. FGBP
1/4 tsp. xanthan gum

Canned fruit? For a vinaigrette? Why yes! There are so many varieties to choose from. My favorite is fruit cocktail. To make this vinaigrette, put everything together. Blend well. If you can your own fruit, that is even better. This makes a great dipping sauce for chicken or pork. Kids will also love it for dipping fruit into. I add no more sugar or sweetener of any kind; it is just great the way it is. Any herb, cayenne pepper, cinnamon, jalapeño, or allspice can be added.

Roasted Garlic (V)

1 c. roasted garlic
1 c. red wine vinegar
2 c. EVOO
1/2 tsp. KS
1 tsp. FGBP
2 tsp. Italian seasoning
1 1/2 tsp. sugar or artificial sweetener
1/4 tsp. xanthan gum

Roasted garlic vinaigrette—what a sweet idea. Oh yeah! Garlic, when roasted, loses that bite and takes on a sweet taste—not overly sweet, just nice. The directions for roasting garlic are in the recipe for **Tomato Roasted Garlic Chive** vinaigrette. I use red wine vinegar in this recipe. If you do not like a strong, pungent vinegar, use cider vinegar or rice wine vinegar. I also use all EVOO for this recipe. If you find EVOO to be too much for your taste, try using half EVOO and half salad oil. If you do not like Italian seasoning, use basil or oregano instead. Put all the ingredients together. Blend well. Use this recipe as a basis to make plenty of other vinaigrettes. You can add fruit, tomatoes, or even vegetables, and replace the oil with vegetable stock to make it fat free.

Fat-Free Blackberry Cranberry (V)

2 c. blackberries (fresh or frozen)
2 c. fresh cranberries or 1 ea. 15 oz. can whole berry sauce
1 c. rice vinegar
2 c. cranberry juice
1 tsp. KS
1 tsp. FGBP
1 tsp. ground cloves
1 tbls. fresh ginger
1/2 c. sugar
1/8 tsp. xanthan gum

This is a fantastic vinaigrette to use for baked ham or roast pork. I prefer to use fresh blackberries and cranberries.

*Cranberries, often referred to as bounceberries, grow wild all over Northern Europe and are grown for harvest in North America in low-lying bogs. They float when they are ripe so the farmers know they are ready to harvest.

If you use fresh cranberries, I suggest increasing the sugar to 3/4 c. Start with the 1/2 c. Blend the vinaigrette, then taste. Add more if needed. I use the fresh ginger because I like the zip it adds to this recipe, ground can be used. If you have not used fresh ginger:

*Ginger/Gingerroot: There are 2 forms, young ginger, found mainly in Asian markets, has a thin, pale skin that does not need peeling, and mature ginger has a thick, rough skin that must be carefully peeled away before using. Make sure the piece of ginger you select is not shriveled or wrinkly. That means it is old and not flavorful. Ginger needs to be cut into small pieces to blend. If it is put in the food processor or blender in a chunk more than 1/2 inch long, it will string and wrap around the blades).

If you use fresh cranberries, from my experience, I find they blend better if they are frozen when used. They are noisy but will blend well. When you decide whether to use fresh or frozen blackberries, fresh or canned cranberries, or fresh or dried ginger, put everything together in a blender, food processor, or in a container to use a handheld blender. Get to blending. This is another vinaigrette that a little cayenne pepper or jalapeño will only add to the flavor and your enjoyment of finding new ways to use it.

Strawberry Blueberry Chocolate (V)

2 c. strawberries (fresh or IQF)
2 c. blueberries (fresh or frozen)
1/4–1/2 c. chocolate syrup
1 c. apple cider vinegar
2 c. salad or canola oil
1/2 tsp. KS
1/2 tsp. FGBP
1/4 c. sugar (optional)
1/4 tsp. xanthan gum (optional)

Who doesn't like chocolate with strawberries or blueberries?

*Chocolate (*xocolatl, *Aztec for "bitter water") comes from the theobroma ("food of the gods") cacao bean, a tropical cocoa bean.*

I sure do. If you use frozen berries, there is no need to completely thaw them before blending. It is a little noisy though. I do not use EVOO in this vinaigrette because I think it takes away from the fruit flavor. If you disagree, then by all means use it. I would make the vinaigrette without the sugar, taste, then add if you think it needs to be sweeter. The same with the chocolate syrup: add more after tasting if you want more. To make this vinaigrette, simply put everything together and blend well. I have no herbs in this recipe, but that doesn't mean you can't add any. I think thyme or basil would go well.

Spicy Blueberry Sweet Italian (V)

1/2 c. sugar
1 c. rice wine vinegar
1 c. EVOO
1 tsp. Italian seasoning
1 ea. Thai chili
1 c. blueberries fresh, frozen even canned pie filling
1/2 tsp. KS
1/2 tsp. FGBP
1/4 tsp. xanthan gum

Sweet Italian Vinaigrette is a recipe from my book *Janie's Simply Entree Salads for Two*. I have incorporated it into this recipe and added the Thai chili and blueberries.

> *Thai chili (TI) a very hot chili that does not lose heat in cooking. They range from green to bright red when ripe. The dried version is referred to as bird chili because when it is dried it resembles a bird's beak shape.*

When using Thai chilies, I suggest you wear gloves. If you cut the chili the long way, then remove the seeds and membranes. It won't be as hot; it will still be hot, but not as much. To make this vinaigrette, put everything together then blend well. (If you use blueberry pie filling, make the recipe without adding sugar first. Taste. Adjust sweetness with 1/4 cup sugar to start. You can always add more, but you cannot take away.) If you do not want to use the Thai chili but want a chili, I suggest you use a jalapeño or, for a smoky flavor, a chipotle chili.

Pineapple Horseradish (V)

4 c. pineapple (fresh or canned)
1 c. rice vinegar
1 tbls. horseradish (prepared or fresh)
1 tsp. KS
1 tsp. FGBP
1 c. salad oil
1 c. EVOO
3–4 tbls. sugar

If you have not used fresh pineapple before, you will need to know how to peel it. Lay the pineapple on its side. Cut off the top and the bottom, revealing the fresh meat. Set up on the bottom. With a sharp knife, cut down between the skin and the meat, following the curve of the pineapple in a sawing motion. Continue to cut in this way all the way around the pineapple. If there are any dark pieces of the skin still on the meat, trim them off. The center core needs to be removed. This can be done by cutting the pineapple in half then, using a V cut, remove from the center of each half. Or, put the pineapple on its bottom and cut down between the core and the meat on all 4 sides to remove the core. Cut into bite-sized pieces.

Horseradish is a root herb that has been around since ancient times. Horseradish is available fresh, and should be firm with no signs of blemishes. Peel and grate. You can also purchase horseradish already prepared in jars in 2 colors: white that is packed in vinegar or red, packed in beet juice.

I would suggest buying already processed unless you like to peel and grate your own. To make the vinaigrette, put everything together and blend well.

Roasted Nectarine Green Onion (V)

6 c. raw nectarine (about 6 whole)
2 c. green onions
2 c. apple cider vinegar or nectarine nectar or juice
4 c. salad oil
1 tsp. KS
1 tsp. FGBP
1/2 c. sugar

Nectarine (nehk-tah-REEN) is related to the peach. The skin is softer and should be a bright golden-yellow with red hints. Nectarines contain vitamins A and C. Use them the same way you would peaches.

To make this vinaigrette, start by roasting the nectarines. To do this, preheat the oven to 350 degrees. Spray a cookie sheet with pan spray, cut the nectarines in half, remove the seeds, and cut each half into bite-sized pieces (or leave whole, your choice). It will be blended. Roast for 10 minutes. Check to see if they are very soft—not mushy, just really soft. Remove from the oven and let cool. Cut the root end off the green onions, then slice them all the way to the end in pieces no bigger than 1/2 inch. If you leave the pieces of green onions too long, they will string and wrap around the blades. Combine everything together and blend well. This is another vinaigrette that is great with some heat added, such as crushed red chilies, jalapeños, or habañeros.

Citrus Red Onion Tarragon (V)

1/2 c. fresh orange juice
1/2 c. fresh lemon juice
1/2 c. fresh lime juice
2 c. red onion
1 tsp. fresh garlic
1 tbls. tarragon (dried or fresh)
3 tbls. sugar
1 tsp. KS
1 tsp. FGBP
2 c. salad oil
1/4 tsp. xanthan gum

This is another vinaigrette that I do not use EVOO, because it takes away from the citrus taste. Grapefruit, tangerine, blood orange, or any other citrus fruit can be used in place of or along with the citrus fruits I suggest. You can also make this fat free or sugar free by replacing the oil with fruit juice and the sugar with a substitute. To make this vinaigrette, put all the ingredients together and blend well. As with all fruit vinaigrettes, some spice can be added for a kick.

Spicy Thousand Island

1/2 c. chili sauce (sweet chili sauce is sold in the stores where Worcestershire sauce is sold)
1/4 c. sweet pickle relish
2 c. canola oil
1/2 c. red onion
1/2 c. rice wine vinegar
1/2 tsp. KS
1 tsp. FGBP
1/2 tsp. Worcestershire sauce
1 tsp. hot sauce
1–2 tsp. cayenne pepper

The difference between this recipe and the **Thousand Island Vinaigrette** recipe in my recipe book *Janie's Simply Entree Salads for Two* is the cayenne pepper I use to make this recipe spicy. If you do not like cayenne pepper, use jalapeños, habañeros, or chipotle peppers.

> *Worcestershire (WOOS-tuhr-shuhr, WOOS-tuhr-sheer): The recipe was created by the English in India. Named after the town it was first bottled in, in Worcester, England. It is made of many ingredients, including anchovies, so it is not vegan; some vegetarians eat fish and chicken. It can make some recipes darker in color, and if you use too much can take over the flavor.*

You will also see there is no EVOO in this recipe. That is because it takes over the flavor of all the other ingredients. To make this vinaigrette, put all the ingredients together but use 1 tsp. of cayenne. Blend well, taste. Add more cayenne to taste, but keep in mind the cayenne flavor will increase in a few days but will peak and not get any hotter after a while.

Strawberry Coconut (V)

2 c. strawberries (fresh or IQF)
1 ea. can coconut milk
1 tsp. KS
1 tsp. FGBP
1 c. rice wine vinegar
2 c. salad oil
1/2 c. coconut
1/4 tsp. xanthan gum

Strawberry again! Why yes, it is such a versatile fruit and goes so well with other fruits.

> *Coconut: native to Malaysia. It is now grown all over the South Pacific and parts of Asia. Coconut has 3 layers: a hard, hairy outer layer, smooth brown layer of skin, and the tender white meat. The center is an opaque liquid center that is delicious to drink.*

Fresh coconut is delicious to eat but a pain to get to. I buy it already processed. It can be found in chunks of fresh or grated and dried. Coconut milk is usually sold where the Asian food is in the market. Before opening, shake the can well and turn upside down to open. The lid will be coated with the thick coconut residue. Scrape that off into the container you are using to blend in. Add the rest of the ingredients and blend well. I did not use an herb in this vinaigrette, but you sure can. I suggest rosemary, thyme, basil, or even dill. In my recipe book *Simply Vinaigrettes from Ancho Chili to White Wine* are recipes for **Coconut Vinaigrette** and **Strawberry Rosemary Vinaigrette**. They both can be made separately then blend some together.

Apple Fig (V)

1 1/2 c. fresh figs
1 ea. red or green apples
1 c. apple juice
1 c. apple cider vinegar
1 tsp. KS
1 tsp. FGBP
1 tbls. sugar or artificial sweetener
1 tsp. ground cardamom
3 c. EVOO
1/4 tsp. xanthan gum

---

*Cardamom (KAR-duh-muhm): This aromatic spice is native to India and is part of the ginger family. It is grown in India, Asia, and Pacific Islands. It can be bought in seed form or already ground. Seed form is the best to buy because it loses flavor after it is ground. The entire pod can be ground and used. Just remember—a little goes a long way.

*Figs are native to Southern Europe, Asia, and Africa. The entire fruit is eaten from the soft skin to the tiny seeds. They range in color from purple-black to almost white. The purple-black are the most common used in the US. There are hundreds of varieties. My grandmother had a fig tree in her backyard, and as a child I would not eat them because I did not like the look of them. Well! You can imagine when I tried them as an adult. They can be used raw or cooked.

To make this vinaigrette, wash the figs then cut into pieces. Wash the apples then cut into pieces, removing core. I do not peel them; I like the tiny bits of skin. Put everything together in a blender or container. Blend well. If you are not sure of the cardamom, use 1/2 tsp. first, taste, then add more if needed. This is an exception to my EVOO rule. All EVOO just goes so well with this recipe. If you do not like EVOO, then use all salad oil or half and half. If you want it fat free, use all apple juice.

Strawberry Pear Red Onion (V)

1 c. strawberries (fresh or IQF)
1 ea. fresh pear (canned, frozen, or dried)
1/2 c. red onion
1/2 tsp. thyme (fresh, frozen, or dried)
1 c. rice wine vinegar
1 c. salad oil
1 c. EVOO
1/2 tsp. KS
1 tsp. FGBP
1/8–1/4 tsp. xanthan gum

Strawberries aren't the only berry good in this vinaigrette. Try blueberries, raspberries, or blackberries. Use the same amount of each or a mix of all of them in place of the strawberries. The pear should be ripe and soft. If you use canned or frozen, use 1 cup. If you use dried, use 2 ea. halves. When you use dried fruit for a vinaigrette, put it in a heatproof container. Heat the vinegar until very hot (not boiling). Pour over the dried pears, then let set for about an hour. Make sure the dried pears and vinegar are at room temperature or cold. Heat will ruin the vinaigrette. I do not peel the pear. You can, if you prefer. I cut the pear in half then into fourths. Cut out stem. Cut each fourth in half and put in a container to blend. If using fresh strawberries, cut off stems. Cut in half and add to pears. Peel and cut the red onion into pieces. Add to pears and strawberries. Add the rest of the ingredients and blend well.

Pumpkin (V)

1 ea. 15 oz. can pumpkin
4 tsp. pumpkin pie spice
1 c. apple cider vinegar
2 c. salad oil
4 tsp. sugar
1/2 tsp. KS
1 tsp. FGBP
1/8–1/4 tsp. xanthan gum

Pumpkin vinaigrette? Are you kidding me? No, I am not.

Pumpkin is actually a fruit, a member of the gourd family, which includes all melons, watermelons, and squash. When the colonists arrived in America the Indians taught them how to use pumpkin, pie being the most popular dish. The seeds are called pepita. Let them dry in the air for a few days, then put on a cookie sheet in a 350-degree oven for 5 to 10 minutes until toasted. Pumpkin seed oil is also available at specialty stores; it is made from the seeds. Pumpkin is a great source of vitamin A.

To make this vinaigrette, simply add everything together and blend well. This vinaigrette will last about 3–4 weeks before the pumpkin molds. This is another vinaigrette that is even better with some habañero or jalapeño added.

Chocolate-Covered Cherry Cordials (V)

1 box or 10 ea. chocolate-covered cherry cordials
1 c. apple cider vinegar
2 c. salad oil
1 tsp. thyme (fresh, frozen, or dried)
1/2 tsp. KS
1/2 tsp. FGBP
1/8–1/4 tsp. xanthan gum

Are you kidding me? Chocolate-covered cherry cordials? Is there nothing she will not make into a vinaigrette? I can think of a few like broccoli, cauliflower, turnips . . . you get the idea.

Place the chocolate-covered cherry cordials in a blending container with the vinegar. Let sit for 1 hour to soften; this makes blending easier. Add the rest of the ingredients and blend well. This will last several months in the fridge.

Chocolate-Covered Blueberry Cordials (V)

1 ea. box chocolate-covered blueberries
1 c. apple cider vinegar
2 c. salad oil
1 tsp. thyme (fresh, frozen, or dried)
1/2 tsp. KS
1/2 tsp. FGBP
1/8–1/4 tsp. xanthan gum

This vinaigrette is made exactly like the **Chocolate-Covered Cherry Cordials** vinaigrette. You can also make a chocolate-covered cherry cordials/chocolate-covered blueberry cordials vinaigrette—just use half the box of each together with the amount of all the other ingredients given in the recipes.

Pomegranate Balsamic and Almond EVOO (V)

1/4 c. pomegranate balsamic
1/2 c. almond EVOO

Where do I find these balsamic vinegars and nut oils? There are stores in most cities that specialize in natural, flavor-infused balsamic vinegars and nut oils, seed oils, and natural herb-, fruit-, and chili-infused olive oils. If you are at the grocery store, read the labels to make sure the product is all natural.

Place the ingredients in a bowl or closed container. Shake or stir until well blended. I like to use 1 part vinegar to 2 parts oil. If your taste is half and half, then by all means mix it to your taste. If you do not use all the vinaigrette on this salad, store in the fridge; it will keep a long time.

Raspberry Chocolate Balsamic (V)

2 c. raspberries (fresh or frozen)
1 c. balsamic vinegar
2 c. chocolate chips or shavings
1 c. salad oil
1 c. EVOO
1/2 tsp. KS
1/2 tsp. FGBP
2 tsp. thyme (frozen, fresh, or dried)
4 tsp. sugar
1/8–1/4 tsp. xanthan gum

> *Balsamic vinegar (bal-sah-mihk vihn-ih-ger) comes from Modena and Reggio Emilia, Italy. The grapes used are white and are cooked down to a dark color. Balsamic is aged in barrels of various woods and reduces in volume naturally. Young aged is 3–5 years, middle aged 6–12 years, and noble aged 13–100 years. If the product is labeled traditional, it must come from Modena, Italy, and be labeled as such. Balsamic vinegars are thick, dark, rich, and some sweetness.*

Once you taste balsamic vinegar, you will not want any other type. To make this vinaigrette, put everything together and blend well. You may not need the xanthan gum because balsamic tends to make thicker vinaigrettes.

Pineapple Tomato Tarragon (V)

2 c. pineapple (fresh or canned)
1 c. rice wine vinegar
1 c. EVOO
1 c. salad oil
2 c. tomato (peeled, deseeded, diced)
1/2 c. red onion
2 tsp. dried tarragon
2 tsp. sugar
1/8–1/4 tsp. xanthan gum

This vinaigrette is a way to use leftover pineapple. If you do not know how to peel pineapple, the directions are in the recipe for **Pineapple Horseradish** vinaigrette.

Rice wine vinegar is made from fermented rice and is lighter in color and has a mild, sweet taste. It is great used in vinaigrettes that are made with fruit. It is found in the Asian food section at most grocery stores.

The directions for blanching and peeling fresh tomatoes is in the recipe **Tomato Mint** vinaigrette. To make this vinaigrette, simply peel and dice the pineapple, or if using canned, drain well but keep the juice for drinking or cooking. The tomatoes—blanch and peel. Cut in half, remove seeds, then dice. If you use canned, drain well. Save the juice for cooking or drinking. Maybe even mix the pineapple juice and tomato juice together to drink. Peel the red onion and cut into small pieces. Put everything together in a container and blend well. Yes, I blend this recipe. You do not have to if you want everything to be chunky. Then, combine everything together and mix well with a spoon. This is another vinaigrette that will not keep for months, because the pineapple and tomato will go bad.

Dinners and
Entree Salads

All the recipes for the salads can be cut in half to make a dinner salad. I do not specify in each recipe which make a great smaller dinner salad; they all do. All the salads that are vegetarian will have a (V) next to the salad name. Any of the salads made with chicken can be grilled, baked, broiled, roasted, or even boiled. I love to use those whole chickens that you can buy at the grocery store that are rotisserie cooked. Any recipe containing chicken can be made with beef or pork. Any salad with beef or pork can be made with chicken. All the salads, of course, can be made vegetarian or vegan. When making salads with fruits, including berries, do not be afraid to add tomatoes. They are actually a fruit but used as a vegetable. I have a lot of salads with fruits and tomatoes in them. They are delicious in a bowl of fruit salad. Any of the salads in this book can be made into wraps. All the vinaigrette recipes are in the **Vinaigrettes** section.

Grape Bacon Banana

3 c. spinach
3 c. baby greens (any variety)
2 c. grapes
1 ea. banana
2 c. strawberries
1 c. grape tomatoes
1 c. cashews
2 ea. 6 oz. chicken breast
1 c. grape bacon vinaigrette

Grapes and bacon? Bacon goes well with everything. I was pouring the grease off the sheet pans I cooked bacon on and it hit me: How would grapes and bacon be together? Well, I tried it and it was awesome. I do not add any more bacon to this salad because the bacon flavor would take over. I want everyone to taste everything in this salad.

To make this salad, start with a mixing bowl. Add the spinach and baby greens, cut the grapes in half, add to bowl, slice the banana, and add to the bowl. Banana? In a salad with bacon? Why yes, it is amazing! Try a bacon, banana, peanut-butter sandwich. Slice or quarter the strawberries. Add them to the party, then cut the grape tomatoes in half and add. Dump in the cashews, then dice the cooked chicken, which can be dark or white meat, baked, grilled, or boiled, cooked fresh for this meal or left over. Add to the bowl. Pour in the dressing. Toss together well. Divide between two large salad bowls or dinner plates. More cashews can be added to top.

Apple Maple
Cayenne Pepper Chicken

Raw chicken breast or thigh, bone in or boneless
Maple syrup
Cayenne pepper
KS
FGBP

This salad is best if the chicken is baked 1 day ahead and allowed to chill overnight. I do not give specific measurements for the above ingredients because it depends on how much chicken you want. If it is bone in, I suggest 1 lb. If boneless, 2–6 oz. Breast or thigh meat will be enough for 2 servings. The maple syrup depends on how sweet and how much maple flavor you like. Cayenne pepper quantity depends on how hot you like it.

Spray a cookie sheet or baking dish with pan spray. Lay in the chicken. Pour 1 tbls. of maple syrup over each piece of chicken, then sprinkle with cayenne pepper, KS, and FGBP. Add about 1/4 c. of water to the cookie sheet or baking dish. Place in a preheated, 350-degree oven. Bake for 15 to 20 minutes until chicken is done. Remove from the cookie sheet or baking pan. Place in another container. Put in fridge to cool overnight to let flavors soak in. Add the following ingredients:

6 c. mixed baby lettuces
1 c. celery
1 c. raisins
1 c. pecans
1 c. apple maple cayenne pepper vinaigrette

Cut the chicken into bite-sized pieces. Place in a mixing bowl. Put the raisins in a bowl, cover with hot water, and let sit 10 minutes to soften. Drain well. Add to chicken. Dice celery and add to chicken, then add pecans. Pour on the vinaigrette. Mix well. Using large dinner plates or salad bowls, put the mixed baby greens on the plates or in the bowls, then top with the chicken mixture. More pecans can be scattered over the salad. Another way to serve this salad is to put everything together in a mixing bowl, toss well, then place on plates or in salad bowls.

Spinach Avocado Chicken

6 c. spinach
1 c. grape tomatoes
1 c. blueberries
1 c. strawberries
1 c. blackberries
1 c. raspberries
1 ea. avocado
2 ea. 6 oz. chicken breast
1/2 c. red onion
1 c. pecans
1 c. bacon avocado vinaigrette

This salad I like to serve in large salad bowls. I also like to marinate the chicken overnight in a spicy blend of crushed red chili and salad oil with salt and pepper. I do not add vinegar, water, or citrus juice. The oil keeps it moist and the red-chili flavor soaks in. Also, by not using any acid or water, if you decide not to cook the chicken for 2 or 3 days it will marinate great. Grill, bake, broil, or panfry the chicken. While this is being done, cut the grape tomatoes in halves. Peel and dice the red onion. Using the paring knife, cut the avocado all the way around from top to bottom. Twist to open. Remove the seed with a spoon. Using a paring knife, carefully make 4 slices from top to bottom inside the skin—not cutting through the skin—then 6 to 8 across the other direction. Use the spoon to remove the meat from the skin. Quarter or slice the strawberries. Add the blueberries, blackberries, and raspberries. Add the tomatoes, red onion, avocado, and berries together. Mix carefully. Do not mash the avocado. To assemble this salad, place half the spinach in each bowl then top with tomato mix. Dice or slice cooked chicken, place on top of salad. Add the pecans, then drizzle with the vinaigrette. This salad can also be tossed together then placed in bowls.

Tomato Mint

6 c. baby greens
1 c. gouda cheese
1/2 c. almonds (plain, toasted, or candied)
1/2 c. red onion
1 c. cucumbers
2 ea. 6 oz. chicken breasts
1 c. tomato mint vinaigrette

Gouda cheese (GOO-dah) has been made in Holland since the sixth century. It represents 60–65 percent of the country's cheese production. It is aged from 1 month to 5 or 6 years. This explains the range of color from pale yellow to deep gold. The flavors range from mild to rich, fruity and nutty.

The chicken can be marinated for 2–4 hours in some of the vinaigrette or overnight in straight oil (vegetable, canola, or olive oil) with fresh mint chopped. No vinegar, because that will cause a chemical reaction with the protein in the chicken and the chicken will start to cook. Never rinse the marinade or brine off of the meat before cooking. To toast the pecans, preheat the oven to 350 degrees, place the pecans on a cookie sheet or in a pie pan, then place in the hot oven. Check after 5 minutes. If they are toasting around the outside edges and not in the center, stir. Return to the oven for no more than 2 minutes, then check again. They should be nicely toasted. Make sure they are completely cooled before adding to the salad.

The directions to candy nuts are in the recipe for **Strawberry Banana Coconut** salad. This is the kind of salad I like to put on large dinner plates and spread it all out. The gouda cheese, I like to dice. It has a rind on it that will peel off nicely with a vegetable peeler, then dice to your desired size, or even shred. When I have onion on a salad (red, white, or yellow), I like to dice it small. How I prepare the cucumber depends on what the salad is. For this salad I would not peel the skin off, but I would cut it down the center and remove the seeds then dice. The decision to peel or not is up to you. I like to grill the chicken, but the choice is yours. To assemble this salad, place the baby greens on the large plates. Spread it out. You can mix the almonds, onions, and cucumbers together, then place over the greens or add each ingredient separately.

Pork and Berries

6 c. baby greens
2 ea. 6 oz. pork loin or 2 c. pulled pork (without the BBQ sauce)
1 c. strawberries
1 c. blueberries
1 c. blackberries
1 c. raspberries
1 c. cucumbers
1/2 c. red onion
1 c. grape tomatoes
1 c. roasted red bell pepper
Roasted Red Bell Pepper El Pato

Pork in a salad with berries? Why not! This is a great way to use leftover pork roast, pork loin, or even pork chops. I also like tomatoes with fruits and berries; after all, tomatoes are fruit. I like to toss this salad together with the pork diced or shredded. To make this delicious salad in a large mixing bowl, add the greens, diced or shredded pork, the strawberries (either sliced or quartered), and the blueberries, blackberries, and raspberries whole. The cucumber I usually dice. First I cut off the ends then cut down the center. I then cut each half down the center, remove the seeds, then dice. You can also cut it in half then slice thin in half-moon pieces. I do not peel my cucumber; I like the skin. The red onion, peel then dice. Add everything together in the mixing bowl. Cut the grape tomatoes in halves, add to the bowl, then add the vinaigrette. Toss well. Place in salad bowls or on large plates. This salad can also be served plated with the vinaigrette drizzled over the top. It is a beautiful salad to see and eat. Leave out the pork and it is a great dinner salad served with a meal of pork with potatoes and green beans.

Nectarine Walnut (V)

6 c. romaine lettuce
1 c. grape tomatoes
1 ea. fresh nectarine
1 c. toasted walnuts
1 c. roasted nectarine green onion vinaigrette

*Romaine (roh-MAYHN) is said to have originated on the Aegean island of Cos. Its dark, hearty leaves are crisp and hold up well to vinaigrettes and dressings. The inner leaves are lighter in color.

When I cut romaine lettuce, I use the outer leaves and the inner heart, as some call it. The ribs are really crunchy and some people cut them away from the leaves. I use them; I love the crunch. To make this salad, use either large salad bowls or dinner plates. The directions to toast walnuts or any nuts is in the recipe for **Tomato Mint** salad. Cut the grape tomatoes in halves or, if they aren't too large, leave whole. The nectarine I cut in half. Remove the seed. Dice into bite-sized pieces.

To make this salad, place the romaine in the center of salad bowls or dinner plates. Scatter the grape tomatoes over the lettuce, then the diced nectarine. To do this, wash the nectarine. You can see the indent all the way around. Run the knife around the edge all the way to the seed. Twist the 2 halves to open. Remove seed, dice, and cover with the walnuts (they are also great candied on this salad. Directions to make candied nuts are in the recipe for **Strawberry Banana Coconut** salad. Then drizzle with the vinaigrette. This is another salad that is great made smaller to be eaten as a dinner salad with an entree of chicken.

Citrus Apple Pear

3 c. romaine lettuce
3 c. baby greens
1 ea. whole orange
1 ea. apple (red, yellow, or green)
1 ea. pear
1/2 c. toasted almonds
2 ea. 6 oz. tuna steak
1 c. citrus red onion tarragon vinaigrette

If you do not like to cut your own lettuce, they are all available precut. A chemical is used in the packaging process to preserve the product; that is why you have a smell. The lettuce can be rinsed in cold water or ice water then dried well, either in a lettuce spinner or on towels. The pieces of precut romaine are sometimes too large, so tear or cut them smaller. Use either large salad bowls or dinner plates. Add the lettuce, either mixed together or one on top of the other. Peel the orange whole. Using a paring knife, cut each segment out from between the membranes and lay on top of the lettuce. The apples can be sliced or diced. If you are not eating the salad right away, I suggest you put the apple and pears in lemon water until ready to use. Then place them on top of the salad. After cooking the tuna steaks, slice them and lay across the salad. Scatter the almonds over the plates. Drizzle with the vinaigrette. Canned tuna can also be used in place of tuna steaks, as well as salmon filets or another fish.

Grilled Vegetables (V)

1 ea. zucchini
1 ea. red onion
1 ea. bell pepper (any color)
1 ea. eggplant
2 ea. tomato (red or green)
1 bunch asparagus
4 c. romaine lettuce
1/2 c. EVOO
1 ea. garlic clove or 1 tsp. chopped garlic
2 tsp. basil (fresh or dried)
KS
FGBP
Balsamic vinegar (any flavor)

The vegetables can be grilled outside over charcoal, gas, or wood, or inside if you prefer. Do not peel the zucchini. Slice in rings about 1/2 inch thick. Peel the onion slice about 1/2 inch thick. (When I grill vegetables, I slice them thicker than roasting. They hold up to the heat and remove from the grill better.) Cut the ends off the bell pepper. Cut down side. Lay open. Remove the membrane and seeds. Cut into 4 pieces. Peel the eggplant, slice, and lay on paper towel or kitchen towel. Salt lightly and let dry off some. Slice the tomato into 1/2 inch slices. Cut the bottom ends off the asparagus; they tend to be tough and woody. Use about the top 4 inches of the stalks. In a small saucepan, heat up the EVOO with the garlic and basil. Lay the vegetables on sheet pans. Coat both sides with the EVOO herb-garlic mix. Salt and pepper the vegetables. Grill to your liking. While they are grilling, cut the romaine into bite-sized pieces. Place onto dinner plates. When they come from the grill, place on 2 dinner plates on top of the romaine. Drizzle with the roasted red bell pepper vinaigrette and the balsamic vinegar. Enjoy. Grilled chicken or pork can be added to the plate as well as fish.

Green Tomatoes,
Berries, and Almonds

1/2 c. almonds
1/2 c. blueberries
1/2 c. raspberries
1/2 c. strawberries
6 c. baby greens
1 c. green tomatoes
1 c. roasted garlic vinaigrette
2 ea. 6 oz. tuna steak, salmon steak, or beef steak

*Almonds are the kernel of the almond tree nut. They are grown a lot in California, the Mediterranean, and Australia. The ones sold in the US are sweet almonds. Bitter almonds are illegal to sell in the US, as they have a poison in them that disappears when they are roasted but cannot be sold here. They are a nutritional powerhouse. Almond oil is made by pressing sweet almonds. The directions to toast nuts are in the recipe for **Tomato Mint**. The recipe to candy is in the recipe for **Strawberry Banana Coconut**.

I use baby greens for this salad. As in any of my salad recipes, you can use lettuces other than baby greens. Each lettuce in the mix of baby greens or spring mix, as it is sometimes called, can be bought separately. They are all full of nutrients. This salad is also a great way to use leftover cooked tuna or salmon.

To make this salad, use either large salad plates or dinner plates. This is another salad that is great tossed together with everything, including the tuna or salmon. To do this, use a large mixing bowl. Put all the ingredients together, including the tuna or salmon. Add the vinaigrette. Toss carefully so you do not mash the berries. I like to slice the strawberries for this salad, plated or tossed.

To plate, put the baby greens in the center of the bowls or plates. The almonds can be toasted, candied, sliced, or slivered. Scatter over the salad. Add the blueberries, raspberries, and strawberries. The green tomatoes I dice. To do this, cut out the core. Cut into slices, then dice. The seeds do not need to be removed; they are not fully developed. I love the taste of green tomatoes; they are crisp with a tart taste. The tomatoes can also be sliced into wedges arranged around the plate. Slice or dice the steak of your choice. Over the top, drizzle with the vinaigrette.

Another way I like to serve this salad is to put the greens on the plate or bowl, cut the core out of the tomato, cut across the tomato—not all the way through. Turn and cut across several more times, making it look like wedges still connected at the bottom. Spread apart. Set on top of the greens. Scatter all the berries and almonds over greens. In a mixing bowl, break up the cooked tuna or salmon. Add some of the vinaigrette mix. Pour the rest of the vinaigrette over the tomato and lettuce. Save some of the nuts to sprinkle over the top.

Strawberry Banana Coconut

3 c. romaine lettuce
3 c. baby greens
2 c. strawberries
1 ea. banana
1 c. almonds (candied)
8 ea. breaded chicken strips (recipe follows)
1 c. shredded coconut (plain or toasted)
1 c. strawberry coconut vinaigrette

To make candied nuts (they all are done the same way), use 1 egg white for each cup of nuts. Preheat oven to 350 degrees. Separate the egg and save the yolk for baking. In a mixing bowl, add egg whites, 1 tsp. cayenne pepper, and 1 tbls. sugar. Mix with an electric mixer or wire whip until almost the consistency of meringue. Add the nuts, mix well, and place on a sprayed cookie sheet. Place in oven for 5 minutes. After 5 minutes, check if nuts are still very moist. Return to oven for no more than 3 minutes. Remove from oven, let cool, then hide so you and family do not eat them before the salad is made. You may want to make extra to store in a ziplock bag to keep crisp for later use. I am sure you have noticed that there are no recipes for iceberg lettuce in this book. I do not care for iceberg, but that doesn't mean you cannot use it. I like romaine and baby greens mixed together. If you find the size of the baby greens, or spring mix, as some call it, too big, then cut them up. It's allowed; the lettuce police won't come get you.

There is coconut in this recipe, and yes, you can toast it. To do this, preheat the oven to 350 degrees. Spray a cookie sheet. Spread the shredded coconut on the cookie sheet. Put in the oven. Do not walk away! Check after 5 minutes. If the outside edge is toasting but not the center, mix outside edges in, return to the oven, and check every minute; coconut will burn easy. Let cool before using. Keep stored in a closed container in the fridge. I keep mine in the freezer, pull out, use what I need, and return to freezer. Toasting increases the sweetness.

This recipe also has breaded chicken strips in it. You can buy frozen premade or make your own.

Breaded Chicken Strips

2 ea. 6 oz. boneless chicken breasts
1/2 c. flour
1/2 tsp. KS
1/2 tsp. FGBP
1/2 tsp. garlic powder or granulated
1/2 tsp. onion powder
1/4 tsp. cayenne pepper (optional)
1/4 c. oil
1 ea. cookie sheet
Pan spray

I do not do the flour, egg, flour. I do not like that much breading on my chicken strips. Preheat the oven to 350 degrees, spray the cookie sheet well, and spread the oil over the cookie sheet. In a mixing bowl, combine all the dry ingredients together or mix well in a ziplock bag. Wash and cut the chicken breasts into 4 pieces each. Toss the chicken strips in the flour mix. Place on the cookie sheet. Put in the oven and cook about 10–15 minutes. Check for doneness. I like to turn half way through. The strips should be crispy and golden brown. Move to a paper towel to remove excess grease.

Now you are ready to make this salad. Again, it can be plated or tossed. I will give the directions to plate. As usual, the choice is yours: large bowls or large plates. Combine the baby greens and romaine, slice or quarter the strawberries, scatter on the salad, and slice the banana between both plates. The chicken strips can be cut into 3–4 pieces each or left whole. Scatter the cut pieces over the salad or lay the whole strips across the salad. Drizzle with the vinaigrette then top with the coconut.

Strawberry Pear

3 c. baby greens
3 c. arugula
1 c. fresh strawberries
1 c. roasted pears
1 c. candied walnuts
6 ea. red onion rings
2 ea. 6 oz. grilled chicken breast or pork loin
1 c. strawberry pear red onion vinaigrette

> *Arugula (ah-ROO-guh-lah) is a bright-green leaf that looks a lot like radish greens (which are very good in a salad also). If the leaves start to turn yellow, they are not very tasty. I love the taste of arugula; it is somewhat bitter with a peppery taste. The leaves should be washed well, dried, and wrapped in a plastic bag or put in a ziplock bag to be used within 2 days. I have chopped the leaves then added to pasta sauce. Yes, it can be used as an herb. Try adding it to sautéed vegetables.*

There are over 5,000 varieties of pears grown around the world. Pears roast really nicely. Preheat oven to 350 degrees. Cut them in halves the long way. Remove the stems then core. Place cut-side up in a baking dish. Sprinkle with KS and FGBP. Place in the oven. Roast for 10 minutes. Check oven; they need to be golden brown and soft but not mushy. You can also drizzle some EVOO on the pears before roasting. You can also grill them cut-side down until marked nicely and soft, not mushy. Make sure that the pears are room temperature or chilled before using. The directions for candied walnuts are in the recipe for **Strawberry Banana Coconut** salad.

My favorite way to serve this salad is to toss. To do this, use a large mixing bowl. Add the baby greens and arugula together, then remove the stems from the strawberries. Slice or quarter the strawberries and add to bowl. Dice the pears and add to the bowl. Add the candied nuts. Dice the chicken or pork loin and add to the bowl. Toss with the vinaigrette. Place in the center of large dinner plates or bowls. Peel and slice the red onion into rings and place on top of the salad. The red onion can also be diced and tossed in the salad.

To serve plated, select either large dinner plates or salad bowls. Divide the baby greens and arugula between the 2 plates or bowls. Slice or quarter the strawberries and place on the greens. Dice or slice the pears and place on the salad. Scatter with the candied walnuts. Slice or dice the chicken or pork. If you dice, scatter over salad. If you slice, cut each breast into 6 slices and arrange around the salad. Peel and slice the red onion and place 3 large rings on each salad, or dice and scatter over salad.

What a beautiful salad! It's almost a shame to eat it. No wait, that is what you made it for. Drizzle with the vinaigrette. If you do not like strawberries, try blueberries or blackberries. This is also a salad that some diced cheese would be awesome on. I suggest a Havarti cheese or sharp cheddar. Cheese makes everything better.

Pumpkin Candied Bacon

6 c. baby greens
12 ea. slices pumpkin pie–spiced candied bacon (recipe follows)
1 c. pumpkin pie–spiced candied pecans (recipe follows)
12 ea. grape tomatoes
1 c. pumpkin vinaigrette
1 c. pumpkin spice croutons

Pumpkin! Pumpkin! Pumpkin! Yes indeed, pumpkin! I hope you love pumpkin like I do. The only meat in this salad is the bacon. That does not mean you cannot add pork or chicken. I think even a nice grilled tuna or salmon steak would be great also. I made this simple salad, but that does not mean you cannot add berries or even bananas. Onion would be good also.

To make this delicious salad, place half the greens in the center of what you are going to serve it on, cut the grape tomatoes in halves or leave whole, then scatter over the greens. Chop the bacon and scatter over salad, then add the pecans and croutons. Drizzle with the vinaigrette, or put everything together in a bowl and toss with the vinaigrette.

Pumpkin-Spiced Candied Bacon

12 ea. thick-sliced bacon
2–3 c. brown sugar
2 tbls. pumpkin pie spice

Preheat the oven to 350 degrees. Use a cookie sheet with a baking rack. Spray well with pan spray; the bacon will stick to rack if you do not. Put the brown sugar in a container that the bacon will lie flat in. Cover each slice generously with brown sugar on both sides. Press with your hands to make sure the brown sugar sticks to the bacon, then sprinkle with the pumpkin pie spice. I suggest you mix the pumpkin pie spice with the brown sugar; that way it is on both sides. Lay the bacon on the rack on the cookie sheet. Place in preheated oven and bake for about 20 to 30 minutes. You want this bacon very crispy with the brown sugar caramelized to it. This bacon is actually better made the day before and left out to dry so it is crunchy. Good luck with waiting for the next day, so maybe make 24 slices—some for now, some for later. If you do not like brown sugar, use white sugar. If you want a little spice, sprinkle some cayenne pepper on the bacon before putting in the oven, or add it to the brown sugar.

Pumpkin-Spiced Candied Pecans

1 c. pecans
2 tsp. pumpkin pie spice
2 ea. egg whites
2 tbls. sugar

The recipe for candied nuts is in the recipe for **Strawberry Banana Coconut Salad**. Unless you want the pumpkin spiced candied pecans to be hot, leave out the cayenne pepper in the recipe to make candied nuts. I would leave the cayenne pepper in the recipe. I love to put jalapeños in pumpkin pie, even habañeros.

Pumpkin Spice Croutons

4 c. diced bread
2 tbls. pumpkin pie spice
EVOO

Day-old bread is the best! I find to use fresh is too soft and smashes when you try to slice. Also, Italian or French bread is the best.

Preheat the oven to 350 degrees. Dice the bread into bite-size or smaller pieces, if you want a large crouton you can pick up with your fingers to eat with the salad. Place the diced bread in a mixing bowl. Add the pumpkin pie spice then drizzle with the EVOO. I do not give amount for the EVOO because it depends on how much oil you like. Not enough there, too dry; too much there, oily. Start with 1/4 c. Add more 1/4 c. at a time until the bread is moist but not wet. Place in the oven for 5 minutes. Check the bread; it should be golden brown and crunchy. If the bread is not golden brown, return to the oven for 3–5 minutes. When golden brown, remove from oven. Let get room temperature before placing on the salad.

Baby Greens and Tomato with Pomegranate Balsamic and Almond EVOO

6 c. baby greens
1 c. diced tomato
1/2 c. pomegranate seeds (if available)
1/2 c. diced red onion
1/4 c. toasted almonds (optional)
1/2 c. pomegranate balsamic and almond EVOO vinaigrette
2 ea. 6 oz. chicken breasts or tuna steaks

Pomegranates?

Pomegranate (POM-uh-gran-uht) is a fruit I grew up eating. They grow well in California and Arizona. They are available in season at most food stores. Pomegranates have a thin-touch skin about the size of oranges. The seeds are all separated by a thin, bitter membrane and take a while to separate. They are delicious and have a tart taste. The juice will stain your clothes so wear an apron or peel and deseed in water.

The directions to toast nuts is in the recipe **Tomato Mint** salad. In the center of each salad plate, add half the baby greens and top with the diced tomato, pomegranate seeds, almonds, and red onion. Slice or dice the chicken. Place on top of the salad, then drizzle with the pomegranate balsamic and almond EVOO vinaigrette. Some of the pomegranate seeds and/or almonds can be sprinkled on top.

Chocolate-Covered Cherry Cordials (V)

6 c. baby greens
10 ea. grape or cherry tomatoes
1 c. toasted pecans
1 c. chocolate-covered cherry cordials vinaigrette

Place the baby greens in the center of the salad plates. Cut the tomatoes in halves, adding 6 pieces to each salad. Sprinkle with the toasted pecans. The recipe for making toasted nuts is in the recipe for **Tomato Mint** salad. Drizzle the salad with the vinaigrette. I have kept this salad simple, because too much takes away from the vinaigrette, but by all means add more, such as cheese, onion, croutons, grilled chicken, or breaded chicken tenders—even grapes or chopped chocolate-covered cherry cordials.

Raspberry Chocolate

6 c. baby greens
2 c. strawberries (fresh or dried)
2 c. blueberries (fresh or dried)
1 c. candied walnuts
1 c. chèvre cheese (goat cheese)
1/2 c. chocolate chips
2 ea. 6 oz. grilled chicken breast
1 c. raspberry chocolate balsamic vinaigrette

Chèvre cheese?

> *Chèvre (SHEHV-ruh, SHEHV): This word is "goat" in French. It is made from white goat's milk and has a tart taste. Pur chèvre is made of 100 percent goat's milk, while mi-chèvre is made of 50 percent goat's milk and 50 percent cow's milk. Very soft, creamy, and spreadable.*

If I am doing a cheese display, I like to take a log of chèvre, roll in dried herbs or chopped nuts, and lay on the display with a knife to slice. The directions to make candied nuts is in the recipe for **Strawberry Banana Coconut** salad. The directions for dried fruit is in the recipe for **Fat-Free Dried Fruit** vinaigrette. This is a great salad for that special occasion such as Valentine's Day, anniversary, bridal shower, or even a baby shower. The chicken breast I like to marinate in EVOO and dry herbs for 1–2 days. While the chicken is grilling, in the middle of two large salad bowls or dinner plates place the baby greens. The strawberries I like to slice. That doesn't mean you cannot cut off the stems. Then, cut in halves, scatter the strawberries on the plate, then add the blueberries, candied walnuts, and chocolate chips. The goat cheese can be sliced or simply dropped in pieces, pulled apart from the log, and placed on top of the salad. The grilled chicken can be sliced or diced and put on top of the salad. Drizzle with the vinaigrette. More nuts and/or chocolate chips can be scattered over the salad.

Sandwiches, Roll-Ups, Wraps, and Flatbreads

Four-Cheese Panini

1 ea. waffle iron
1 ea. small wheel of brie
1/4 lb. muenster cheese slices
1/4 lb. or small piece of gouda cheese
1/4 lb. sharp cheddar cheese slices
1/2 c. melted butter
4 slices ea. bread of your choice
Sliced tomatoes (optional)
Sliced onions (optional)
Green chilies (sliced or diced) (optional)
Roasted red bell peppers (optional)

Plug in the waffle iron. Let it get hot. Melt the butter. Lay the bread flat. Spread the melted butter on all 4 slices. Open the wheel of brie cheese. Slice as thick as you like. Yes, you can eat the skin. If you buy the gouda in a chunk, slice it the same way. It is available sliced in some stores, or the deli will have it sliced for you. The sharp cheddar is available everywhere. Lay 1 or 2 slices of bread in the waffle iron; it depends on the size of the waffle iron. Layer the cheeses. If you are adding the optional ingredients, they can be put between the layers of cheese or on top of the cheese. Close the iron and cook for at least 5 minutes. Open cover. If longer is needed, close again for about another 3 minutes.

Tomato Ricotta Cheese Hoagie

2 ea. tomatoes (red, yellow, or orange)
2 c. ricotta cheese
1 tbls. basil or oregano (fresh or dried)
2 ea. roasted bell peppers (red, yellow, orange, or green)
1 ea. red onion
2 ea. crunchy hoagie rolls
1/2 c. melted butter

Use a griddle or skillet to toast the hoagie rolls. Do this by turning heat on to griddle or under skillet. Split the hoagie rolls down the center in halves. I like to remove some of the bread in the center so it isn't so filling. Brush the cut sides with the melted butter. Lay on griddle or in skillet. Let cook until nicely toasted. If I remove some of the bread from the center, I press down on the hoagie rolls to toast the centers. When the rolls are toasted, remove from griddle or skillet. Spread with the ricotta cheese mixed with the basil or oregano (or both) generously, then layer with sliced tomatoes.

The tomatoes can also be put on the griddle or skillet to cook some. If you do this, spray the griddle or skillet with pan spray. The onions can also be cooked with the tomatoes.

Add the onions and roasted bell peppers. Red, yellow, or orange bell peppers roast very well. Green doesn't because green is not ripe yet. All bell peppers and chilies are green until they ripen. The recipe for roasting bell peppers is in the recipe for **Antipasti Display**. Dice or julienne cut the bell peppers. Place the top piece of the hoagie on, then cut in half, then enjoy.

Other ingredients can be added to this hoagie such as mild chilies, jalapeños, olives (black or green), banana peppers, and other cheeses.

Italian Meats and Cheeses Roll-Ups

1 tube premade pizza dough
1/4 lb. pepperoni
1/4 lb. salami
1/4 lb. provolone cheese
1/4 lb. mozzarella cheese
Optional ingredients: sliced onion, sliced tomato, sliced bell pepper, sliced mushrooms, pepperoncinis, pizza sauce or alfredo sauce, Italian seasonings

I use the premade pizza dough in the tube, like biscuits. Sprinkle a flat surface with flour. Lay out the pizza dough. Sprinkle with flour. Using a rolling pin, flatten out to about 1/8 inch. If you leave the dough as it is out of the tube it will be too thick. You can cut the piece of dough in half for smaller roll-ups, or leave whole for larger. If you are using a sauce, spread it on the dough, then lay out the pepperoni, then top with provolone, then layer salami, then mozzarella cheese. Roll up. Put on a cookie sheet sprayed well. Place in a preheated, 350-degree oven for about 15 to 20 minutes until the dough is golden brown and crunchy.

Fruit, Berry, and Vegetable Wrap (V)

2 ea. large flour tortilla
1/2 c. raspberries
1/2 c. blueberries
1/2 c. strawberries
1/2 c. blackberries
1/2 c. cucumbers
1/2 c. red onion
4 ea. slices tomato
2 ea. leaf of lettuce
1/2 c. fat-free mixed berry vinaigrette
2 ea. fish filets or chicken breast (optional)

This wrap can be made vegetarian or with fish, chicken, pork, or beef, used warm or cold. To make this wrap, heat the tortilla on a griddle or in the microwave; it is easier to handle. Lay on a flat surface. Place the lettuce leaf at the bottom of the tortilla. Add 2 tomato slices. Layer the cucumbers, onions, then the berries. If adding fish, chicken, pork, or beef, add now. Pour the vinaigrette over all. Fold the bottom of the tortilla over everything. Fold in sides. Roll up securely with sandwich picks cut in halves. Serve on large dinner plates with a side of cottage cheese.

Strawberry Chipotle Chicken Wrap

2 ea. large flour tortilla (any flavor)
2 ea. herb-marinated grilled chicken breast or leftover chicken
2 c. baby greens or fresh spinach
2 ea. slices tomato
1/2 c. strawberries
1/2 c. blueberries
1/2 c. red onion
1/2 c. nuts (your choice)
1 c. strawberry chipotle vinaigrette
4 ea. frill picks

Warm the tortilla—either on a griddle, skillet, stove, or in microwave—just until warm, about 30 seconds. Any longer and they will become hard. This is a great way to use up leftover chicken—baked, boiled, fried, roasted, grilled . . . you get the idea. Lay the tortillas on a flat surface. Toss the baby greens or spinach in just enough, maybe 1/4 c. of the vinaigrette. Place this half on each tortilla toward the bottom. Lay on the chicken. Cut the tomato slices in halves. Lay 2 halves on each tortilla on the chicken. Slice the strawberries. Put half on each tortilla, then add the blueberries. Slice or dice the red onion. Add to tortillas. Put half the nuts on each tortilla. Fold this over. Tuck in the stuffing. Fold in the sides, then finish rolling. Put in frill picks to keep together. Enjoy. Use the rest of the vinaigrette to dip wrap in.

Pork Pineapple Horseradish Wrap

2 c. baby greens
2 ea. 6 oz. pork loin or 2 c. pulled pork (no sauce or tossed in some of the vinaigrette)
1/2 c strawberries
1/2 c. blueberries
1/2 c. raspberries
1/2 c. pineapple (fresh or canned)
1/2 c. red onion
1/2 c. cucumber
2 ea. slices tomato
1 c. pineapple horseradish vinaigrette
2 ea. large flour tortillas

My mouth is watering just writing this recipe. Who would have thought of putting pineapple and horseradish together? Why, me, of course.

To make these wraps, start by grilling or roasting the pork loin. The pulled pork can be hot or cold; which one you choose is up to you, but toss the pork in some of the vinaigrette. Let set to marinate while you prepare the rest of the ingredients. The day before is even better. Chicken can be used instead of pork. Heat the tortilla in the microwave for 30 seconds or on a griddle. Slice the pork loin very thin. Slice or quarter the strawberries. Peel and dice the red onion. The cucumbers can be peeled or not (I do not peel them), seeds in or deseeded. To deseed, cut down the center. Scoop out the seeds. Slice thin. To make these wraps, lay the tortillas on a flat surface. Toss the baby greens in some of the vinaigrette. Place half on the tortilla in the center of the bottom half. Add all the other ingredients. Cut the tomato slices in halves. Lay 2 pieces end to end. Drizzle more vinaigrette over the top. Too much will make the tortillas mushy. Fold over the sides toward the center, then fold over the bottom part of the tortilla over the ingredients, then roll up. Cut in half. Place both halves of each wrap on plates.

Fork-and-Knife
Flatbread Ham and Egg

2 ea. pita or flatbread
2 tbls. dijon mustard
8 ea. slices ham
2 ea. chilled hard-boiled egg
12 ea. grape tomatoes or 1 ea. whole lg. tomato
1/2 c. diced red onion
2 c. fresh spinach
1/2 c. spicy Thousand Island vinaigrette

Who does not like ham and eggs? This is a nice meal for a day by the pool, baby shower, or bridal shower. You can also set this up as a build-your-own buffet along with a bowl of fresh fruit along with short cake and whipped cream for dessert.

To make this fork-and-knife flatbread (I give you the choice of pita or flatbread in these recipes because some may not like flatbreads), start by heating a griddle or skillet on medium heat. Spread the dijon mustard on the pita or flatbread. If you do not like mustard, use some of the vinaigrette. Lay mustard-side down on griddle or skillet. Cook to a golden brown. This will take 2–3 minutes. When they are nicely toasted, place on 2 plates. Toss the spinach in the spicy Thousand Island vinaigrette. Place on top of the pita or flatbread, then lay the ham on top of the spinach, then slice the eggs. Lay on the ham (poached or fried eggs can be used instead), then add the tomatoes. If you use the grape tomatoes, cut them in halves; they will stay on sandwich better. Or, slice the tomato. Lay 2 slices on each pita or flatbread, then peel and dice the onions. Scatter over the top or slice in rings to place on top. Drizzle more of the vinaigrette over the top. Other ingredients can be added, such as sliced banana peppers, jalapeños, even roasted bell peppers. A cheese can be added also, sliced or shredded, such as swiss, provolone, even cream cheese! Spread on the pita or flatbread after toasting.

Mozzarella Tomato Berries Chicken Flatbread

2 ea. pita or flatbread
1 c. fresh tomato
2 c. fresh mozzarella cheese
2 c. baby greens
1/2 c. strawberries
1/2 c. blueberries
1/2 c. raspberries
2 ea. 6 oz. chicken breasts
1 c. apple fig vinaigrette

Fresh mozzarella (maht-suh-REHL-lah/moht-suh-REHL-lah): This is a very soft mozzarella cheese usually made with cow's milk. It originally came from Italy and was made from water buffalo milk. You can still buy it made from water buffalo milk at specialty cheese stores and cost more. Fresh mozzarella is packaged in whey or water so it does not dry out. If you do not use it all, make sure you store it in water in the fridge. I have had it both ways—made with cow's milk and buffalo milk. I prefer the buffalo milk.

This dish is a great way to use up leftover chicken. You do not have to use grilled chicken filets; chopped or shredded thigh meat or leg meat will also work. To make this, first decide if you want to use a pita or flatbread. You can toast the pita or flatbread. I give the directions to do this in the recipe **Fork-and-Knife Flatbread Ham and Egg**. Place the pita or flatbread on 2 large dinner plates. Toss the baby greens in the vinaigrette. Place on the pita flatbread, then top with the chicken, which can be tossed in some of the vinaigrette also. Slice the fresh mozzarella. Place on top of the chicken. At this point if you want to place this under the broiler to melt the cheese some, place the pita or flatbread on a cookie sheet first. Put under the broiler for 1–2 minutes. The cheese will become golden brown on the top but will not completely melt. Remove from the oven. Return to the plates. Slice the tomato. Add 2 slices to each, then scatter with the fresh berries. Drizzle with more vinaigrette.

Spinach Pesto Flatbread

2 c. spinach pesto (recipe follows)
2 ea. roma tomatoes (or tomatoes of your choice)
1 ea. red onion sliced thin, sautéed
2 ea. balls of fresh mozzarella cheese
1/2 c. melted butter
Cookie sheet

Preheat the oven to 350 degrees. Brush the melted butter on both sides of the flatbread. Place on the cookie sheet. Put in oven for 3–5 minutes. Remove from the oven. Set aside to cool. Leave oven on. Slice the onions very thin. In a skillet, add some oil or butter. Add the onions. Sauté until they are tender and translucent. Remove from skillet. Let cool. Remove the fresh mozzarella from the water it is stored in. Slice each into 4 or 5 slices. Slice the tomatoes into 5 or 6 slices. Spread the spinach pesto on the flatbread, then add onions and tomatoes. Top with sliced cheese. Place in the oven for about 5 minutes, until cheese gets golden brown and bubbly. Serve whole or cut into 2 or 4 pieces.

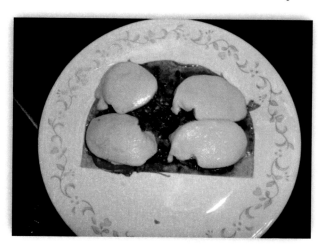

Spinach Pesto

1 lb. fresh spinach
1 c. nuts (pine nuts, pecans, walnuts, almonds—the choice is yours)
1/4–1/2 c. EVOO
1 c. shredded parmesan cheese
1 tbls. fresh garlic
1 food processor or blender

Add the ingredients, except the EVOO, in the blender or food processor. Turn on processor. Slowly add the EVOO. Start with 1/4 cup (which is 4 tbls.). Blend until well blended but not dry. Too much oil will ruin it and cause an oily mess. More can be added but not taken away.

Sauces and Au Jus

Rhubarb Sauce (V)

4 c. rhubarb
1/4 c. water
1/2 c. sugar, honey, or artificial sweetener

Wash the rhubarb. Slice from tip to end in pieces about 1/2 inch wide. Put everything together in a pot. Let cook until well done. Stir often; it will burn on the bottom of the pan if not watched well. I do not use a thickener for this sauce; it thickens on its own. Taste for sweetness. Add more sugar, honey, or artificial sweetener to suit your taste. Citrus zest and/or juice can be added for a different flavor, as well as cinnamon, jalapeño, or an herb can be added as well.

Roasted Garlic Cream Sauce (V)

1/2 c. roasted garlic (at least 4 bulbs roasted) or 1/2 c. roasted whole
garlic cloves
2 tbls. butter
1 c. heavy cream
1/2 tsp. KS
1/2 tsp. FGBP

To roast the garlic, preheat oven to 350 degrees. Roasted garlic
can be bought at some food stores all ready to use. Roasted
garlic you make is much better; it doesn't have the preservatives
in it. Use whole, unpeeled garlic bulbs (this is the cluster of unpeeled
garlic cloves still attached together). Already-peeled garlic cloves
can be used. Unpeeled are better flavor, in my opinion. The
bulbs can be left whole or cut in half through the center, making
2 halves. The unpeeled cloves are cooked by placing the garlic
in a baking pan or garlic roaster in the oven for 10 minutes.
Check to see if cloves are soft and mushy. If not, return to oven
for another 5 minutes. Test again. If garlic is done, remove from

oven. Let cool before handling. If you are roasting peeled garlic cloves, toss in EVOO. Place in baking dish in hot oven for 10 minutes. Test for softness. Return for 1 minute at a time only. They will burn really easily. Let cool before mashing. To remove garlic from whole cloves, cut bottom off bulb then squeeze out garlic. Measure garlic. Heat a saucepan. Add butter, melt. Add garlic. Turn heat low so butter doesn't burn. When butter and garlic are hot, add heavy cream. Let simmer until desired consistency. A small amount of flour can be added to butter and garlic to make a roux (the recipe for making roux is in the recipe for **Cream of Chicken Noodle Soup**. I prefer the flavor of the sauce without the roux. The sauce can be cooked a few days ahead. Reheat slowly when used. Serve the sauce either under the beef medallions, on top of, or on the side.

Roasted Red Bell Pepper Sauce (V)

2 ea. red bell peppers
1 tsp. fresh garlic
2 tbls. butter
1/2 c. chicken stock or broth
1/2 tsp. KS
1 tsp. FGBP
Cornstarch (slurry) (optional)

The directions for roasting bell peppers is in the recipe for **Antipasti Display**. To finish the sauce, put the peeled bell peppers in a blender. Puree well. Melt butter in a saucepan. Add garlic you have chopped. Sauté until tender. Add pureed roasted bell peppers. Add chicken stock or broth (the recipe for making chicken stock and broth is in the **Soups** section of this book). Reduce heat. Let sauce reduce by half. A small amount of cornstarch mixed with water or chicken stock can be added to thicken; this is optional. The instructions for making slurry are in the recipe for **Mushroom Au Jus**. Yellow bell peppers or orange bell peppers can be used instead of red bell peppers. Green bell peppers are not ripe yet and will not peel very well. If you want to use them, roast, clean, then blend, but you need to strain them to remove the skin. All bell peppers start out green. As they ripen they turn either red, yellow, or orange. This is also true with jalapeños and most other chilies.

Mushroom Au Jus

1 c. sliced mushrooms
1/2 tsp. Italian seasoning
1 ea. stalk celery
1 ea. carrot
2 ea. garlic cloves
1/2 ea. onion
4 c. beef broth
1/2 tsp. KS
1/2 tsp. FGBP
4 tbls. unsalted butter
1–2 tbls. cornstarch (slurry)

Remove the stems from the mushrooms. Cut the carrot, skin on, into 5 or 6 pieces. Cut celery stalk in 5 or 6 pieces. Cut onion in half. Leave skin on. Cut into 4 pieces. In a 1 qt. stock pot, melt the butter over medium heat. Add the mushroom stems, carrots, celery, onions, garlic cloves, and Italian seasoning. Let this sauté for about 5 minutes, stirring often. You do not want it to burn. Add the 4 c. beef broth. Let simmer to reduce to half. While this is reducing, slice the mushrooms thinly. When the broth has reduced, turn off heat. Using a strainer, strain the broth, being careful not to lose any of it or burn yourself. Return the broth to the pot. Add sliced mushrooms and slurry. The vegetables can be discarded or fed to the dog. Let the broth come to a slow boil. Add the salt and pepper.

> *Slurry: the mixture to thicken hot dishes, such as soups, sauces, and stews, no matter what you use, such as cornstarch, flour, or arrowroot, mixed with a liquid of water, juice, or broth. Mix 1 tbls. of cornstarch with enough water to make a paste. Slowly add to the broth, mixing constantly. For some reason, there is not a ratio I can find of amounts of cornstarch to water to get the exact blend. It is mind boggling. I suggest you start with 1 tbls. cornstarch to 2 tbls. water. I find the same thing happens with flour.*

Turn heat down. Let simmer. This is an au jus. It should not be thick like a gravy or sauce, just barely coating the spoon. To make this au jus vegetarian, replace the beef broth with vegetable stock.

Mushroom Beef Sauce

1/2 c. mushrooms (your choice)
1/2 c. onion (your choice)
1 tbls. chopped garlic
2 tbls. butter or EVOO
1 tsp. dried rosemary
1 c. beef stock
1/4 c. red wine (optional)
1 tbls. cornstarch ("slurry"—the recipe for making this is in the recipe for **Mushroom Au Jus**)
1/2 tsp. KS
1 tsp. FGBP

If the mushrooms have any particles on them, wipe with a damp cloth if needed. Never put mushrooms in water to wash. They are like sponges and will soak up water. Slice or cut in quarters mushrooms. Peel and slice very thinly or dice onions. In a skillet or sauté pan, add butter or EVOO or both. Let butter melt or oil heat up, never to smoking point. Add mushrooms and onions. Let sauté until tender. Add garlic and rosemary. Salt and pepper can be added any time in any quantity you like. If you are adding wine, do so now. Let reduce until almost gone. Add the beef stock (the recipe to make stock is in the **Soups** recipes). Let simmer until reduced about a quarter. Slowly add cornstarch slurry, stirring constantly. Let simmer until the thickness you like. If you like it thinner, add less. If you like it thick, add more after at least 5 minutes of simmering. This sauce can be made several days ahead then reheated for use. If it gets too thick, thin with more beef stock, never water; it dilutes the taste. Tomato juice or a fruit juice can also be added for flavor. To serve, pour over foil dinner right in foil.

Beef Gravy

1 qt. beef broth
1/4 c. roux (the recipe for the roux I like to use for gravy is in
the recipe for **Cream of Chicken Noodle** soup)
Salt and pepper to taste

In a saucepan, heat up the beef broth. When it starts to boil,
turn down to medium. Stir in roux well. If 1/4 c. isn't enough,
add more roux 1 tsp. at a time until thick enough for you. If it is
too thick, thin with 1/4 c. more beef broth. If you feel 1/4 c. is too
much liquid to thin to your satisfaction, then do 2 tbls. at a time,
stirring well. Let simmer for a few minutes. Small amounts of
liquid and/or roux at a time only. If you want a creamy, milk-type
gravy, add about 1/2 c. of milk, half-and-half, or cream. Stir well.
You may have to add more roux—1 tsp. only.

Chicken Dijon Sauce

1 tbls. dijon mustard
1 tsp. chopped garlic
1 tsp. thyme (fresh, dried, or frozen)
KS
FGBP
1 tbls. butter
1 1/2 c. chicken stock
1/4 c. white wine (optional)
1 tbls. cornstarch (slurry) (the recipe to make this is in the recipe
for **Mushroom Au Jus**)

In a sauté pan, melt butter. Add garlic and thyme. Let sauté
about 2 minutes. Add dijon mustard, chicken stock, salt, and
pepper. Let simmer until reduced by half. Add slurry. Let simmer
until thickened. If it is too thin, add more slurry. If it is too thick,
add more chicken stock, never water; it dilutes the sauce. If you
do not like thyme, try basil or oregano. This sauce also can be
made several days ahead. Apple juice or another fruit juice is
also great in this sauce, using half juice, half chicken stock.

Cherry Sauce (V)

1 ea. sweet canned cherries (use liquid) or cherry pie filling
1 tsp. ground sage or rosemary or both
1–2 tsp. cornstarch (slurry) (the recipe for making this is in the
recipe for **Mushroom Au Jus**)
2 tbls. sugar (optional)

In a saucepan on medium heat, add the canned cherries or
pie filling (if using pie filling, do not add the cornstarch or sugar;
it is already in it). Add the ground sage or rosemary (or both). Let
come to a simmer slowly so it doesn't burn. When hot and starting
to bubble some, add the slurry 1 tbls. at a time. Let cook for 5
minutes. If too thin, add the other 1 tbls. of slurry. Mix well. Let
simmer another 5 minutes to cook the starch taste out of the
sauce. Make sure to stir a lot. Do not walk away; it will burn.

Swedish Meatball Sauce (V)

4 c. pineapple juice
2 c. crushed pineapple
2 c. brown sugar
2 c. ketchup
2 tsp. salt
3 tsp. black pepper
1 tbls. Italian seasoning
2 tbls. cornstarch (optional slurry) (the recipe for making this recipe is in the recipe for **Mushroom Au Jus**)

In a pot over medium heat, add all the ingredients together. Stir well. When it comes to a boil, turn heat down. Let simmer for 30 minutes. If you want the sauce thicker, add the slurry to sauce. Let cook at least 5 minutes. If the sauce is still too thin for you, add more slurry. This sauce will soak into the meatballs while in the oven, so cornstarch slurry may not be necessary. It is your choice. Crushed red chilies, jalapeños, or habañeros can be added for extra zip. This sauce is also great on chicken or pork.

Green Tomato Sauce

4 c. green tomatoes
1 c. onion (white, yellow, or red)
2 tbls. sage (fresh or dried)
2 tbls. basil (fresh or dried)
2 tbls. thyme (fresh or dried)
2 tbls. garlic
3 tbls. sugar
2 tsp. KS
3 tsp. FGBP
2 c. chicken broth (the recipe for making broths is in the **Soups** section)
1/2 c. EVOO

Sage (SAYJ): This herb is native to the Mediterranean, where it is used for both culinary and health benefits. The name comes from the Latin word salvas, *meaning "safe." That refers to the plant's healing powers. This is a pungent herb with a slightly musty mint taste. There is also a variety named pineapple sage, and as its name says, it has a slight pineapple taste and smell.*

I chose green tomatoes from my garden that were just on the verge of turning red, yellow, and orange, fairly soft, not hard. Yes, I have all three colors of tomatoes in my garden. I did not blanch them to remove the skins or remove the seeds. The skins are very thin, soft, and cook well. The sage, basil, and thyme came from my garden fresh. Wash the tomatoes and herbs very well. I cut out the stems, then dice the tomatoes into bite-sized pieces, peel and dice the onion, and chop the herbs. If you use whole garlic cloves, chop. If you have a whole garlic bulb, separate, peel, then chop.

In a large saucepan add all the ingredients. Let come to a boil. Turn down the heat. Let simmer for at least 1 hour. I use a hand blender to completely blend the sauce. The tomatoes cook too soft, almost to a mush. Blend very well. Taste the sauce, then adjust the flavor you want. By this I mean add more herbs, garlic, salt, and pepper. I found 3 tbls. of sugar was enough to take away the tart, acidic taste from the tomatoes. I love the crisp, clean taste of green tomatoes. I use them just like I do regular ripe tomatoes.

This sauce can be used in so many different ways: pizza, pasta, dipping sauce for chicken or pork. Add green chilies for a spicy flavor. Try adding diced carrots and celery for a heartier sauce.

Mornay Sauce (V)

2 c. béchamel sauce (this sauce is in the recipe for **Cream of Chicken Noodle** soup in the **Soups** section)
1/2 c. swiss cheese
1/2 c. parmesan cheese

*Mornay sauce (mohr-NAY) is a béchamel sauce that cheese is added to, usually swiss and parmesan.

In a saucepan sprayed well with pan spray on low heat, add béchamel sauce. Stir well. Let slowly get hot, but not boiling; it will burn. Add the swiss cheese, either shredded or diced, and parmesan cheese grated works best. Stir constantly until hot and cheese is melted. A double boiler works great for this sauce to make and keep it warm. This is another sauce that crushed red chilies or jalapeños can be added to.

Relishes and Condiments

These relishes and condiments are a great addition to any salad bar, deli bar, burger bar, or on any salad, sandwich, or burger. They will keep for months and only get better over time. The quantities can be increased as much as you want to make. As with most relishes and condiments, some dried red chilies, jalapeños, or habañeros can be added.

Sauerkraut Relish (V)

2 c. sauerkraut
1 ea. lg. carrots
1 ea. stalk of celery
1/4 c. white onion
1/2 ea. green bell pepper
1 tbls. sugar
1/4 c. apple cider vinegar
1 tbls. caraway seeds

I made this recipe on a dare. I was given some sauerkraut left over from a hot dog buffet and asked if I could make something useful out of it. Without hesitation, I said, "Yes, I can."

Sauerkraut (SOW-uhr-krowt) is German for "sour cabbage." It was not created by the Germans, but is Chinese, created over 2,000 years ago. It was originally made of shredded cabbage and rice wine vinegar. Now it is raw, shredded cabbage combined with salt and/or spices left to ferment.

I walked into the walk-in cooler and started pulling out raw vegetables. I rinsed the sauerkraut very well, then put it in a strainer, drained well, and pressed out all the liquid I could. I then peeled the carrot, cut the celery into 1/2-inch pieces, peeled the onion, and used 1/4 of it, which measured out to 1/4 cup. I then cut the stem out of the bell pepper, cut the pepper in half, removed the seeds and membranes, then cut into small pieces. I used a food processor, added all the vegetables except the sauerkraut, chopped coarsely, then added the sauerkraut, sugar, vinegar, and caraway seeds. I gave it a few pulses. You can make this as chunky or as fine chopped as you like. I removed from the food processor into a storage container, mixed by hand well, put on the lid, and let sit in the refrigerator for a week, then used on sub sandwiches. I have also used this as a condiment for a salad bar and deli bar. Do not be afraid to add crushed red chilies or jalapeños. For color, try adding red bell peppers instead of green bell peppers. Salt and pepper is always optional.

Olive Relish (V)

1/4 c. black olives
1/4 c. green olives
1 tsp. basil
1 tsp. oregano (fresh, dried, or frozen)
1 tsp. thyme (fresh, dried, or frozen)
1/4 c. red bell peppers
1/4 c. green bell peppers
1/4 c. yellow bell peppers
1/4 c. cauliflower
1/2 c. red wine vinegar
1 c. EVOO
1 tsp. garlic
1/2 tsp. KS
1 tsp. FGBP

This relish is best chopped in a food processor—not pureed fine, chopped! If you like it a little more chunky, chop with a knife. If you are using a food processor, drop olives in whole; the bell peppers, simply cut off the top and bottom. Do not throw away. Cut the meat away from the stem, discard the stem, cut into pieces, cut bottom piece up, cut the bell peppers down the side, open up carefully with a paring knife, remove the membranes and seeds, and lay the meat of the peppers open. Cut down center, making 2 pieces the long way. Cut into about 1-inch pieces. Add to the food processor. Remove the cauliflower florets from the stem. Add to processor. The stems, if not tough, can be cut up and added also. If you are using whole garlic cloves, add to processor. If using already chopped, add when combining the rest of the ingredients. Chop coarsely. Remove from food processor into mixing bowl. Add the rest of the ingredients. Mix well. Refrigerate before using.

This is a great addition to sandwiches and subs of all kinds. This mix can also be strained, removing oil and vinegar, then mixed into sour cream for a vegetable dip or added as is to a salad bar.

Green Relish (V)

1/4 c. white onion
1 c. cabbage
8 ea. tomatillos
1/2 ea. green bell peppers
1 ea. stalk celery
1/2 c. apple cider vinegar
1 c. salad oil
1 tbls. sugar
1 tsp. celery seed
1 tsp. mustard seed

*Tomatillos (tohm-ah-TEE-oh): a fruit native to Mexico belonging to the tomato family. Also referred to as a Mexican tomato. They are small, round, and green, covered with a thin, parchment paper–type covering. I wash them in cold water to remove the parchment covering. It is sticky under it. The taste is tart with hints of lemon, apple, and herbs. The texture is very firm, like a green tomato. If ripened fully, they become yellow in color. The seeds are very tiny; do not need removal.

To make this relish I use a food processor. Peel and cut the onion into bite-sized pieces. (As you prep each vegetable, put them in the food processor.) Peel the outside layer off of the cabbage. This is usually thicker than the inner leaves. Cut off a piece of the cabbage. Measure 1 cup. Add to processor. Cut the bell pepper in half, remove the stem, seeds, and membranes, and cut into pieces. Add to rest. Cut celery in 1/2-inch pieces. Add to rest of ingredients. The vinegar, oil, sugar, and seeds can be added now. Process until blended to your liking. If you do not have a food processor, all these relishes can be chopped by hand then mixed well together.

Icebox Pickles (V)

4 c. cucumbers
1 ea. red onion
1 ea. green bell pepper (optional)
2 c. white vinegar (or more to cover)
1/2 c. sugar
1 tbls. poppy seeds

Icebox pickles are also referred to as freezer pickles because they are made the same way, just kept in the fridge, not freezer. You can keep them in the freezer. Thaw as needed. They are sweet, tart, and delicious on salads, sandwiches, or all alone.

> *Poppy seeds: a very small seed dried from the poppy plant with a crunchy texture and nutty flavor. Used in a wide variety of baked goods, dressings, and Asian and Middle Eastern cooking. They are a grayish blue in color and need to be kept dry and in a sealed container.*

To start, wash the cucumbers to remove the wax. Do not peel unless you have an issue with the skin. Slice them very thinly, almost as thin as you can, with or without seeds. I leave the seeds in for myself at home. I have worked in kitchens where the chef wanted them cut in half, deseeded. Put in the container you are going to store them in. Peel the onion. Either cut in half or leave whole. Slice very thinly. Add to cucumbers. The bell pepper needs to be sliced very thinly with seeds and membranes removed. Add to the rest. Mix the vinegar, sugar, and poppy seeds together. Pour over the mixture carefully. Stir. If there isn't enough liquid to cover the cucumber mix, add more, mixing 1/2 c. at a time. I do not add salt to this; it doesn't need it. I have added crushed red chilies for extra kick. Seal container. Refrigerate overnight. The cucumbers take on the vinegar really well and fast. Artificial sweetener can be used instead of sugar. I love vinegar. If you find it too strong, then cut it with water or apple juice.

Mustard Cauliflower (V)

1 ea. head cauliflower (fresh only)
4 c. apple cider vinegar
1 c. white wine (optional)
1 c. dijon mustard
1/2 c. pickling spice
1/2 c. honey
1 ea. large saucepot

This is one condiment that you won't want to be without for a salad bar once you taste it. The finished product needs to set in the fridge for 1 week to cure. I start out by selecting a large, very firm head of cauliflower with no blemishes. Using a large pot on the stove over medium heat, add the vinegar, dijon mustard, pickling spice, and honey. The white wine is optional.

Dijon (dee-ZHOHN) comes from the town of Dijon, France. The color of this mustard is usually grayish-yellow, and has a sharp taste going from mild to hot depending on the seeds used.

Let come to a boil. Turn heat down to just a simmer. Just before you are ready to pour over the cauliflower, turn off heat. Using a sharp paring knife, cut the florets away from the stem. (Don't throw the stem away; cut up and use in salads. Cook, mix with broccoli, or cut up and use in this dish.) Place the cauliflower in a heat-safe container. Carefully pour the hot liquid over the cauliflower. Keep your head back, because if you breathe in the steam it will take your breath away. Stir. Let sit until room temperature. Cover up in the fridge. If you need to be sugar free, there is sugar-free honey available. If you do not like honey, then use sugar. The taste will definitely be different, but it should be just as good. I have never made it with sugar.

Jalapeño Pickled Vegetables (V)

1 ea. jar pickled jalapeños (whole or sliced) (liquid included)
2 c. cauliflower florets
2 c. whole black olives
2 c. zucchini (sliced or diced)
2 c. raw carrots (sliced)
2 c. baby corn
4 c. apple cider vinegar
2 tbls. cayenne pepper (or to taste)
1 ea. large saucepot

Open the jar of jalapeños. Pour liquid and peppers into the saucepot. Put on the stove.

Cayenne pepper (KI-yehn) originated in French Guyana. Made from grinding a variety of hot peppers together into a powder. It is also called red pepper.

Add the vinegar. Bring to a boil. Turn down heat. Pick a fresh head of cauliflower with no blemishes. Cut from the stem as in the **Mustard Cauliflower** recipe. The stems can be cut up and used or saved for other dishes. Cut the cauliflower into bite-sized pieces. Put in a heat-safe container, open. Drain the black olives. Drain off the liquid (this is just water). Add to the cauliflower. Leave the skin on the zucchini. Slice thinly or dice thinly. Add to the container. Peel or do not peel the carrots; that is up to you. Slice them very thinly (if you have a food processor with a slicing blade, that is perfect for this). Add to the rest. Open the baby corn, drain. Add to the rest. Carefully pour the boiling-hot liquid into the container. Mix well. If you need more vinegar to cover heat, then add. Let this mixture completely cool. Cover and put in the fridge. Let set 1 week before using.

I have used this mixture with pasta to make a cold pasta salad. I suggest using cheese tortellini. I buy it frozen at the store already cooked, so add the marinated vegetables to the pasta while it is frozen. Let set overnight. This way, the tortellini will not break apart while mixing carefully by hand. This spicy pickled-vegetable mix is great served with grilled brats or dogs.

Pickled Beets with Hard-Boiled Eggs (V)

2 ea. cans red beets (sliced or whole) or fresh, roasted beets (recipe follows)
Beet juice from cans
2 c. apple cider vinegar
2 tbls. pickling spice
1 tbls. crushed red chilies (optional)
6 ea. peeled hard-boiled eggs (optional recipe follows)
1 ea. large saucepan

Here is the recipe for making these pickled beets with canned beets. In a saucepan, add the juice from the canned beets along with the vinegar, pickling spice, and crushed red chilies (if using). Heat until coffee-hot, not boiling. If you are making this recipe with fresh, cooked beets, add the vinegar, pickling spice, and crushed red chilies (if using). Heat until coffee-hot, not boiling. In a heat-safe container, add the beets. Pour the hot liquid in carefully. Let sit until at room temperature. Add the peeled eggs. Cover. Put in the fridge for 1 week before using. If you add the boiled eggs when the liquid is still hot, it can overcook the eggs.

Roasted Beets (V)

6–8 ea. fresh, whole beets
1/4 c. EVOO
1 c. water
1 tbls. KS
1 tbls. FGBP
1 ea. baking dish (deep enough that beets don't stick up over the top)
1 piece aluminum foil

Preheat oven to 400 degrees. Wash the beets. Cut off ends. Put beets in baking dish. Add oil, salt, and pepper. Mix beets until they are coated with the oil, salt, and pepper. Add water. Cover with foil. Put in oven and bake for 90 minutes. Remove from oven. Carefully open foil. Using paring knife, check for doneness. If knife goes into beets easily, it is done. Remove from oven. Let sit, covered, for 1 hour. If they are not done, return to oven, adding 1/2 c. water if dry for another 30 minutes. Remove from oven. Let sit, covered, for 1 hour. Carefully uncover foil. Remember, they are still warm. Using a paring knife, peel the skin off. It should be loose enough that they peel easily. Slice or dice. Add to the hot liquid (the directions for making the hot liquid is above in the recipe for **Pickled Beets with Hard-Boiled Eggs.** Before you pickle them, take a taste and see how sweet they are. You may never buy canned beets again. I like them hot with butter as a vegetable.

Hard-Boiled Eggs (V)

6 ea. raw, whole eggs
1 qt. water
1 medium saucepot
Ice water to chill

Place the raw eggs in the saucepot. Add the water, making sure the eggs are fully submerged. Place on high heat. When water comes to a full boil, turn off heat. Cover pot. Let sit 12 minutes. After 12 minutes, you can either dump a lot of ice into the pot to shock the eggs to stop the cooking, pour eggs and boiling water over ice, or drain pot and put eggs in ice water. Let sit until eggs are cold. To peel, carefully crack eggs on 1 side against a hard surface. Roll in hands to loosen peel. Remove peel. Rinse eggs. You may want to make extra. I love fresh, boiled eggs.

Smoked Hard-Boiled Eggs (V)

6 ea. hard-boiled eggs
Enough cider vinegar to cover eggs
2 tbls. liquid smoke (or eggs smoked over wood)
1 tsp. garlic (chopped or whole cloves)
1 tsp. FGBP or peppercorn

To make your own smoked eggs on the grill, start either a wood fire or a charcoal fire in a grill with a lid. Soak wood chips in water. Hard-boil the eggs, peel, and put them in a metal pan, such as a metal pie pan. When the wood fire or charcoal fire is ready, remove the wood chips from the water. Place on the wood or coal fire. Place pan of eggs on grill. Close cover. Let smoke for at least 30 minutes, longer if possible, possibly 1 hour. The vinegar does not need to be heated; the eggs absorb the vinegar and smoke very well. Put the smoked eggs in a container large enough to hold 6 eggs. Cover the eggs with the vinegar. Add the garlic and pepper. If you are not using eggs you have smoked but plain, hard-boiled eggs, add all the ingredients together with the liquid smoke. Let set for 1 week before eating. Crushed red chilies or jalapeños can be added.

Spiced Mandarin Oranges (V)

1 qt. canned mandarin oranges
All the mandarin orange juice in the cans
2 tbls. ginger (fresh, dried, or candied—not ground)
1 ea. cinnamon stick
1 tsp. cloves (whole or ground—preferably whole)
1 tsp. nutmeg (fresh grated, if possible)
1 ea. medium saucepan

Mandarin oranges (MAN-duh-rihn): Clementine is the most commonly used. The size varies from the size of an egg or as large as a small grapefruit. The skin is very loose and peels easily. Some varieties are sweet; some are tart. Also, some have seeds, some don't.

Open the cans of mandarin oranges. Drain the juice into the saucepan. Add the ginger. If you use fresh, peel with a paring knife, then chop finely or into pieces. Add the cinnamon stick, cloves, and nutmeg. Put the mandarin oranges into a heat-safe container. Let the juice come to a boil. Turn off. Let come to room temperature. Pour over the mandarin oranges. Cover. Put in the fridge for 1 week before using. This is great served over grilled fish, chicken, or pork.

Feta Cheese and
Olives with Rosemary (V)

2 c. feta cheese
1 ea. can black olives or kalamata olives
1 tbls. fresh rosemary
1 c. EVOO
1 ea. red bell peppers
1 tbls. black peppercorn

> *Feta (FEHT-uh): This cheese is one of the world's oldest,
> originating from Greece and other Balkan countries. Greece is
> the only country that makes true feta cheese and can call it
> that. Feta is made mainly of sheep's milk, but can have
> up to 30 percent goat's milk. It also contains 45–60 percent
> milk fat. The texture is firm and crumbly. It is stored in
> a brine that helps maintain the texture, color, and tangy
> flavor.*

Feta is bought in any grocery where imported cheeses are
sold. Feta is made all over the world, but only feta from Greece
can be called feta. I cannot tell you what names they use, but
you can be sure feta will be somewhere in the name. It will not
say authentic feta. If you do not use all the feta but do not keep
the liquid, store the remaining in water in a closed container in the
fridge. You will find many uses for this cheese: omelets with bacon
and spinach, salads, pizzas, burgers, sandwiches, and appetizers.
This recipe is great with a salad bar, burger bar, or sandwich bar.

Now, on to the recipe. Cut the feta cheese into bite-sized pieces
and put in a mixing bowl. Drain the olives and cut in halves.
Remove the fresh rosemary from the stems. Chop with a knife.
What an aroma! Your whole house will smell like rosemary.

Cut the ends off the red bell peppers. Cut the pepper down the
side. Lay flat. Cut off membranes. Remove seeds. Dice very small.
Add olives and rosemary to the cheese. Put the peppercorn in a
ziplock bag and hit with a rolling pin or heavy pan. Do not pulverize;
give them about 4 hits. If you have a grinder that has the size of

the grinds, use the largest. Add the EVOO to the rest of the mix, blending well. Cover. Put in the fridge. It is ready to use but gets better over several days. The cheese will last like this about 1 week, then it starts to break down, so make in small batches. Have fun finding new ways to use this recipe.

Vegetables

Sautéed Vegetables (V)

12 ea. asparagus spears, or
2 c. zucchini, yellow squash, and onion
1 tsp. garlic
2 tbls. EVOO
KS
FGBP

If you use asparagus, cut off ends. Place in boiling water with salt. Blanch for 2 minutes only. Remove from boiling water. Place in ice water to shock (this stops the asparagus from cooking more).

If you use zucchini and yellow squash, do not peel them. Cut off ends. Cut in half the long way. Slice 1/4 inch thick. Peel onion. Cut in half. Slice and toss with zucchini and yellow squash. Peel and chop garlic. Heat sauté pan. Add EVOO. Add garlic. Cook 1 minute. Toss in vegetables. Sauté until done. A small amount of chicken stock or other liquid can be added. Make sure you add kosher salt and pepper.

Cheese-Stuffed Zucchini (V)

1 ea. very lg. or 2 reg. zucchini
1/2 onion
1 c. shredded parmesan cheese
2 tsp. FGBP
2 tbls. unsalted butter
Baking dish
Pan spray
(Optional additions: diced tomato, bell peppers, mushrooms, blue
cheese, feta cheese, or any other cheese or vegetables you would
like to add. Fresh or dried herbs such as thyme, oregano, basil,
and Italian seasoning can also be added, as well as ground pork,
sausage, or ground beef.)

Preheat the oven to 350 degrees. Wash the zucchini.

*Zucchini (zoo-KEE-nee) is a member of the squash
family and is available year-round at most grocery stores.
The skin color ranges from dark green to light green and is
completely edible. The flesh is pale green and the seeds are
edible. It is used in many vegetarian dishes such as
vegetarian lasagna, where the ends are cut off and the whole
zucchini is used instead of lasagna noodles.*

Dry. Cut off stem and ends. Slice in half the long way.
Carefully remove the center with the seeds and some of the meat
of the zucchini. Leave at least 1/4 inch of meat intact. By the
way, do not peel. A spoon works great for cleaning out the
center. Do not throw this away; it is used as part of the stuffing.
Yes, the seeds are edible. Chop this up along with the onion and
any other items you want to add. Mix with the black pepper. In
a sauté pan, melt the butter. Add the vegetable mix without the
cheese. Sauté until tender. Drain on paper towel; this will
prevent your dish from being too watery when cooking and
serving. Let this mix cool, then add half the cheese. Place the
zucchini halves in the baking dish. Fill with the vegetable mix.

Top with the rest of the cheese. Bake for 30 minutes. This dish can be turned into an entree by simply adding either cooked or raw ground beef, turkey, chicken, or pork with the vegetable mix before stuffing. If you like it a little spicy, no matter what you stuff it with, add some jalapeños or dried, crushed red chilies, or use canned diced tomatoes with chilies. Make sure you drain them well.

Roasted Stuffed Chayote (V)

1 ea. chayote
1/2 onion
1 c. shredded cheddar cheese
1/2 c. bread crumbs
2 tsp. FGBP
2 tbls. unsalted butter
1/4 c. water
Baking dish
Pan spray
(Optional additions: diced tomato, bell peppers, mushrooms, blue cheese, feta cheese, or any other cheese or vegetables you would like to add. Fresh or dried herbs such as thyme, oregano, basil, and Italian seasoning can also be added to the blend, as well as ground beef, pork, or sausage.)

Preheat the oven to 350 degrees. Wash the chayote.

Chayote (chi-OH-tay) is often referred to as a fruit, but it is a member of the squash family with a thin, pale-green skin with a white flesh that needs a lot of seasoning because it is very bland. It was a favorite food of the Aztecs and Mayans. I use it as a vegetable, cooked and raw. It is also great served raw in salads or on vegetable displays.

Dry. Cut in half the long way. Carefully remove the seeds and some of the meat of the chayote. Leave at least 1/2 inch of meat intact. A Tomato Shark or paring knife works great for cleaning out the center. Do not throw this away; it is used as part of the stuffing. Chop this up along with the onion and any other items you want to add. Mix with the black pepper. In a sauté pan, melt the butter. Add the vegetable mix without the cheese. Sauté until tender. Drain on a paper towel; this will prevent your dish from being too watery when cooking and serving. Let this mix cool, then add half the cheese. Place the chayote halves in the baking dish. Fill with the vegetable mix. Top with the rest of the cheese. Add 1/4 c. water to steam. Cover with foil. Bake for 30 minutes. This dish can be turned into an entree by simply adding either cooked or raw ground beef, turkey, chicken, or pork with the vegetable mix before stuffing. If you like it a little spicy, no matter what you stuff it with, add some jalapeños or dried, crushed red chilies, or use canned diced tomatoes with chilies. Make sure you drain them well.

Jalapeño Scalloped Corn (V)

1 ea. can creamed-style corn
4 ea. whole eggs
1 c. bread crumbs
1 tbls. diced jalapeños (canned or fresh, not pickled)
1 tsp. KS
2 tsp. FGBP
1/4 c. milk
4 tbls. butter
Baking dish
Pan spray

*Jalapeño (hah-lah-PEH-nyoh) is a smooth, dark-green turning bright-red, yellow, or orange pepper when ripe. The heat ranges from hot to very hot. Jalapeños are named after a city in Mexico called Jalapa. Most of the heat is in the seeds and membranes inside the chili. To remove them, simply cut the pepper from end to end in half. Remove the seeds and, using a paring knife, cut off the membranes. If you have very delicate skin, wear gloves when handling any chili pepper. Make sure you wash your hands with warm water and soap. Rubbing salt on your wet hands helps, as well as lemon juice. Do not touch your eyes or lips when handling any chili pepper before washing your hands, but still be careful; it may burn even after washing. Jalapeños are full of flavor, adding a nice kick to any dish.

*Scoville scale: In 1912, a man named William Scoville developed a system for measuring the heat in chili peppers. He did this by using people to taste-test the heat levels of sugar water with the extract from the chili peppers. The amount of sugar water was increased until there was no heat detected. This test is named the Scoville Organoleptic Test. At the high end of the scale is 15,000,000 to 16,000,000 Scoville heat units, at the lowest end being a bell pepper at 0 Scoville units. A regular jalapeño chili *ranges from 2,500 to 8,000. The habañero chili ranges from 100,000 to 300,000.*

To make this dish, preheat the oven to 350 degrees. Spray the baking dish with pan spray. Melt the butter, but do not let it burn. In a mixing bowl, add the cooled melted butter, cream-style corn, and diced jalapeños (they can be bought canned diced or whole). To dice, cut in half, remove seeds, and cut off membranes, then cut into thin strips to dice. Add the bread crumbs; this is to soak up the extra moisture. In a small mixing bowl, crack the eggs then whip with a fork. Add to bowl with corn and jalapeños. Add the KS, FGBP, and milk. Mix well. Pour into baking dish. Place in the oven and bake for 45 minutes. This scalloped corn will puff up as the eggs cook and should be eaten right from the oven. As it cools, the liquid will separate and really is not good reheated. If you like heat but do not like jalapeños, try cayenne pepper. Other ingredients can be added, such as cheddar, Monterey jack, or pepper jack cheese.

Honey Cumin
Roasted Cauliflower (V)

4 c. cauliflower florets (fresh or frozen)
1/2 c. pure honey
2–4 tbls. ground cumin
2 tsp. KS
2 tsp. FGBP
1/2 c. EVOO (or oil of your choice; flavored EVOO can also be used)

Cauliflower (KAWL-ih-flow-uhr) is a member of the cabbage family. The name comes from the Latin caulis, meaning "stalk," and floris, meaning "flower." Cauliflower comes in 3 colors: white (the most common), purple, and green. Sometimes the white will have a slight shade of green or purple. Cauliflower is made up of tiny bunches of florets on stalks. These are called curds. Curds? Isn't that a cheese byproduct? Yes, it is, but it is also the name for the pieces cut off the core that we call florets. Cauliflower can be eaten raw or cooked. It is also great steamed or boiled then added to potatoes when mashing them. The green leaves on the base are also edible but have a stronger taste and take longer to cook. No matter how you eat it, choose a head that is firm with no blemishes.

Any of the colors of cauliflower can be roasted or eaten raw. Preheat the oven to 350 degrees. Using a paring knife, cut the florets off the stalk. Rinse in cold water. Drain well. In a mixing bowl, add the rest of the ingredients. Toss well. Spread on a cookie sheet. Put in the oven. Roast 30 minutes or until golden brown. Crushed red chilies can also be added, as well as cayenne pepper for a kick. Roasted cauliflower also makes a great soup. Just roast it, put in a soup pot with chicken stock, add garlic if wanted, let simmer for about 30 minutes, then put in a blender or use a hand emulsifier. Blend well (you might want to save some florets to add to soup after blended). Return to the pot.

Add milk, cream, or half-and-half, then add some cornstarch slurry to thicken. Taste. Adjust seasonings. Also, cheese can be added.

Corn-Stuffed Roasted Tomato (V)

2 ea. lg. tomatoes (any variety) (any color)
1 c. whole kernel corn (fresh, frozen, or canned)
1/2 c. red onion
1 tbls. garlic
1 tsp. KS
2 tsp. FGBP
1/2 c. grated parmesan cheese
1/2 c. EVOO (any flavor)
1 ea. sauté pan
Balsamic vinegar (any flavor optional)

If you use fresh corn, cut it off the cob then blanch it first. Preheat the oven to 350 degrees. Cut the core out of the tomato. Make sure not to cut too deep; just remove what is needed. Cut the tomatoes in halves. Remove the seeds. You can use a spoon or your finger to do this. Throw them away; they're not good for anything unless you dry them to plant. Using a paring knife, cut out the membranes. If you use canned corn, drain well. Peel then small-dice the red onion. If you are using garlic cloves, chop well. Put the skillet on the stove over medium heat. Add 1/4 c. EVOO. When it is hot, but not smoking, add the red onion and garlic. Let sauté until tender. Add the corn, KS, and FGBP. Sauté until it is hot. Place the tomatoes in a baking dish. Put corn mix in the center—1/4 c. in each. Top with the parmesan cheese, then drizzle with the rest of the EVOO. Drizzle each piece with the balsamic vinegar. Put in the oven. Bake for 30 minutes, or until the cheese is a golden brown and tomatoes are cooked. This is also a great dish to use green tomatoes. Cauliflower and/or broccoli can be used instead of corn. Blanch the florets. Drain. Sauté with the rest of the ingredients, then stuff tomatoes and bake.

Potatoes, Pasta, and Rice

Twice-Baked Potatoes (V)

2 ea. lg. baking potatoes
4 tbls. butter
1/4 c. heavy cream
1/2 c. shredded cheese (your choice) (optional)
1/2 tsp. KS
1 tsp. FGBP
EVOO

Select large bakers. Wash well. Dry. Coat with EVOO then sprinkle well with KS. Preheat oven to 400 degrees. Place potatoes on a baking sheet in oven for 45 to 60 minutes. Test for doneness. They need to be well done. Remove from oven. Let cool for at least 10 minutes. Handle carefully. Cut in half long way. Using a spoon, remove the meat from the center, leaving at least 1/4 inch of meat on skin for support. Put removed potato in a mixing bowl. Add butter, heavy cream, salt, and pepper. Mash until well blended. Return to potato shells, using either a spoon or pastry bag. Top with cheese, or cheese can be mixed into potato mix with more added on top. Place back on cookie sheet. Return to oven for about 10 minutes to melt cheese on top. Any other ingredients you want to add can be mixed with potato mix before returning to skins. Green onions, bacon, roasted garlic, jalapeños, or anything else you can think of can be added to potato mix or placed on top.

Mashed Potatoes (V)

1 lb. potatoes (white, red, Yukon gold, etc.)
2 qt. pot
1 c. milk, cream, or half-and-half
1/2 c. butter
1 tsp. KS
1 tsp. FGBP

Peeled or unpeeled, the choice is yours. I love skin on lumpy mashed. If I use large, white potatoes, I usually cut them into 8 pieces; red skin 1/4, same with Yukon gold. If they are small, I leave them whole to boil them. Bring the water to a boil. Some people add salt to the water; all this does is cause the water to boil faster at a higher heat. Put the potatoes into the pot. Cover. With the water, turn heat on high. Let come to a full rolling boil, then let cook for 15 to 20 minutes. Some potatoes can even take 30 minutes. Check for doneness by inserting a paring knife into the potatoes. When they are done, drain in the sink into a colander. Put back into the pot. Add the milk, butter, salt, and pepper. Using either a hand masher or an electric mixer, mash away. If more milk is needed, add small amounts at a time. Chicken or beef broth or stock can be used to cook the potatoes instead of water, or used to mash instead of milk. For a change of taste, try adding dried chives, fresh or dried herbs, horseradish, roasted or fresh garlic, parmesan cheese, or sharp cheddar. I have even added blue cheese. May I suggest adding jalapeños? Cream cheese makes a very creamy, great-tasting mashed. Add about 1/2 c. Another healthy alternative to potatoes is to use turnips or cauliflower instead of, or mashed in with, potatoes. To do this, steam or boil the turnips or cauliflower. Drain. Add to the potatoes then mash.

Dutch-Oven
Scalloped Potatoes (V)

Also can be baked in oven

2 c. potatoes (sliced thin)
1 c. diced onion
2 tbls. flour
2 tbls. chopped garlic
4 tbls. grated parmesan cheese
1 qt. whole milk
1 tbls. FGBP
2 tsp. KS
1 12-inch cast-iron Dutch oven (or 1 baking dish)
Aluminum foil
12–14 small pebbles (go in bottom of Dutch oven under foil)
Hot coals (24 on bottom, 14 on top)

Wash the pebbles. Place in bottom of Dutch oven. Line inside with 2 layers of foil. Wash and slice potatoes thinly. Skin on, skin off, your choice! Me, I leave skin on. Layer 2 c. potatoes in bottom of Dutch oven. Peel and dice the onion. Spread 1 c. over potatoes generously. Use salt and pepper. Sprinkle flour, parmesan cheese, then garlic over potatoes and onions. Add another layer of potatoes, onions, salt, pepper, flour, parmesan cheese, and garlic. Pour milk over all. Make sure the foil is below lid level so lid will seal. Carefully place on top of hot coals. Add coals to the top on lid. Let cook 1 hour. Carefully lift lid. If there seems to be too much liquid, let cook another 10 minutes with lid off.

Rosemary Roasted
Red Potatoes (V)

8 ea. red-skin potatoes (This is medium size. If you use baby size, they're about the size of a quarter. Use 12 or more.)
1 tbls. fresh rosemary
1 tsp. chopped garlic
1 tsp. FGBP
1 tsp. KS
1/4 c. EVOO or salad oil

Fresh rosemary? Yes! If you only have dried, that will work as well. The reason I use fresh is the aroma is released into the potatoes as they cook and the rosemary dries out. Fresh rosemary does not work in foods that have already been cooked, like a cold potato salad with a rosemary vinaigrette. Rosemary in its fresh state takes on the texture of gravel if you chop it to mix with something already cooked.

Preheat the oven to 400 degrees. Wash the potatoes, dry, and either cut into quarters, halves, or leave whole. Put the potatoes in an ovenproof baking dish. If you use fresh rosemary on the stem, lay on top of the potatoes or pull the leaves off the stems. Add the garlic, KS, FGBP, and oil. Toss well. Put in the heated oven. Cook for 30 minutes. Check potatoes for doneness using a knife or fork inserted in a few of the potatoes. If they are not done, return to the oven for 10 more minutes, then check again. The potatoes should be very soft with a crispy outside. If you do not like rosemary, then use basil or thyme, fresh or dried.

Cheese Tortellini Sautéed in EVOO (V)

2–4 c. cooked cheese tortellini
1/4 c. EVOO
1/2 tsp. KS
1 tsp. FGBP
1/4 c. fresh basil (dried can be used; the taste of fresh is just so much better)
1 c. shredded parmesan cheese (to garnish)

If you are using the dry, boxed tortellini, cook according to directions on the box until done. Drain well. If you are using the precooked frozen tortellini, let thaw before sautéing; it is already cooked. Place a large skillet (tortellini needs lots of room to move around or it will break into pieces) on the stove over medium heat. Let get hot. Add EVOO. Add tortellini and basil after EVOO gets hot but not smoking. Be careful: EVOO can get too hot and burst into flames. Sauté for about 2–3 minutes until it is nicely coated with the hot EVOO and starts to turn golden brown. Don't forget to add the salt and pepper. Pour out onto a large plate. Sprinkle with the shredded parmesan. If you are not a fan of parmesan cheese, may I suggest blue cheese?

Pasta Primavera (V)

1 lb. box of pasta (your choice)
2 tbls. dried or fresh herbs (your choice) (basil, oregano, sage, thyme, rosemary)
1/4–1/2 c. EVOO
1 c. onion (red, white, or yellow)
1 c. mushrooms (button, shitake, crimini, portabella, or oyster) (any combination)
1 ea. bell pepper (red, green, orange, or yellow)
1 c. zucchini
1 tsp. KS
2 tsp. FGBP
4 ea. cloves of garlic or 1 tbls. chopped garlic
Pan spray
Large skillet
Large pot of boiling water

Primavera (pree-muh-VEHR-uh) is an Italian word meaning "spring style." It literally means adding raw or cooked vegetables to another dish such as pasta, making it pasta primavera.

Bring 4 qts. of water to a boil. Add pasta. Cook until al dente.

Al dente (al-DEN-te) translated from Italian means "to the tooth," or a little over half done—not fully cooked or mushy.

While pasta is cooking, peel and cut the onions into bite-sized pieces, or julienne cut. Slice the mushrooms about 1/4 inch thick. If they look dirty, you can rinse them if you are using them right away. If you are prepping them a day ahead, wipe with a damp cloth only. Dice or julienne cut the bell peppers. If the zucchini is large, cut off ends and cut down center, then cut into a half-moon shape or quarter, then cut into bite-sized pieces. If it is no bigger around than a quarter, just slice about 1/4 inch thick. The garlic can be fine chopped or coarse chopped, your choice. The herbs can be fresh, dried, or frozen. Just before the pasta is done, in the large skillet add the EVOO. The amount depends on you—how much you want. You want enough to coat the bottom of the skillet well. Add the garlic and onion. Sauté. Let cook about 5 minutes. Add the rest of the ingredients except the pasta. Stir. Let sauté about another 5 minutes. Drain the pasta. Toss in with the veggies. Mix well. Add some salt and pepper to taste. Pour into pasta bowls. Enjoy.

Some shaved parmesan or cheese of your choice can be put on top of the pasta. To make this a nonvegetarian meal, just add some chicken, pork, beef, or fish of your choice. This dish is not limited to the veggies I have used. Add what you like: eggplant, tomatoes or chilies, chayote, and broccoli.

Vegetarian Spanish Rice (V)

1 c. uncooked white or brown rice (1 c. does not seem like enough, but remember—it doubles in volume when cooked)
2 1/2 c. tomato juice
1/2 tsp. KS
1 tsp. FGBP
1 tsp. garlic
1/2 c. onion (white, red, yellow, or green)
1/2 tsp. cayenne pepper
1/2 tsp. cumin
1 ea. jalapeño (red, yellow, orange, or green)
1/2 c. celery

Celery? Really? Yes, I love the taste of celery in Spanish rice.

Celery: In the medieval days, celery was used for medicinal uses. The shorter inner stalks are called the heart. To me, they have the best flavor; they are sweeter and tender. Celery is grown in bunches called stalks. The color should be pale green, with crisp stalks and not withered leaves. The leaves are also very tasty and can be used like the stalks.

A rice cooker is great for making this dish. Make sure you spray the inside well. If you are using a large pot, spray well with pan spray, put the rice uncooked in the pot, and add the tomato juice, KS, FGBP, cumin, and cayenne pepper. Chop the garlic if you have not bought already chopped. Peel and finely dice the onion. Add to the pot. The jalapeño can be left whole or finely chopped. The celery, I like to use the hearts. Pull away the outside stalks to get to the tender heart. Slice the long way through the heart stalks, then dice finely. Also try chopping some of the leaves. Add this to the pot. Mix together well. Now place the pot on the stove over medium heat with a lid on the pot. When the contents start to boil, turn heat down to low. Simmer for 30 to 45 minutes. Stir every 10 minutes. Of course ground beef, pork, or chicken can be added to make this a full meal.

Rice Primavera (V)

1 c. uncooked rice (white or brown)
2 c. vegetable broth or water
1 c. broccoli
1/2 c. green onion
1 c. bell peppers (red, green, orange, or yellow)
1 c. carrots
1 ea. lg. garlic cloves or 1 tsp. chopped garlic
1 tsp. KS
1 tsp. FGBP
1/4 c. EVOO
1 tsp. Italian seasonings
2 qt. saucepan
Pan spray

This is a meal in itself. I especially like to serve this dish with grilled or baked fish.

Carrots: a root vegetable that is a great source of vitamin A. Also a member of the parsley family. The tops should be bright green and moist. The orange color should be bright. Carrots should be crisp, not withered. If you purchase them with the tops on, remove right away. Store in a plastic bag.

To make this rice dish, start by cutting the florets from the broccoli stems. I like to peel the stems with a vegetable peeler, then dice to add to the rice. The green onions I slice from top to bottom, using the entire onion. I dice the bell peppers into 1/4-inch pieces. The carrots I do not peel; there are a lot of vitamins in the peeling. You can peel if you prefer. If the carrots are not over 1/2 inch around, I slice them; if larger, I cut the carrots in half the long way, then each half again, then dice. If they are not too round, I slice into circles. If I use whole garlic cloves, I like to slice thin.

In a 2 qt. saucepan sprayed well with pan spray over medium heat, I add the EVOO. Let it get hot, but not smoking. Add all the vegetables and garlic. Sauté until just tender. Add the broth, rice, Italian seasoning, FGBP, and KS. Mix well. Cover. Let come to a boil. Turn down heat to low. Cover. Let simmer 25 to 30 minutes or according to package directions. Stir well. Enjoy.

Herb and Cheese Rice (V)

1 c. raw rice (white or brown)
1 1/2 c. vegetable stock (the recipe for vegetable stock is in the recipe
for **Stock** in the **Soups** section) (if you do not have vegetable
stock, water can be used)
1 tbls. garlic
2 tsp. basil (fresh, dried, or frozen)
2 tsp. oregano (fresh, dried, or frozen)
2 tsp. thyme (fresh, dried, or frozen)
2 tsp. FGBP
1/2 c. milk, cream, or half-and-half
1–2 c. cheese of your choice (cheddar, parmesan, romano, American,
just to name a few)

**Brown rice is the whole grain of rice with only the outer husk
removed. The light-tan, nutty, chewy texture is from the nutritious
high-fiber coating. The shelf life of brown rice is shorter than
white rice; about 6 months. Also, it takes about 15 minutes
longer to cook. It is also available in quick cooking and instant
rice that cooks much faster. Yes, you can use quick-cooking
white or brown rice, as well as instant rice, in all the rice
dishes I have given you recipes for. Brown rice can be used
in any recipe that calls for white rice. All rice should be
stored in a tight container away from moisture and sunlight.*

I like to make this recipe in the oven. In fact, I prefer to cook
all my rice dishes in the oven. Preheat the oven to 350 degrees.
Using a 2 qt. ovenproof baking dish sprayed well with pan spray,
combine all the ingredients together. Cover with foil. Seal well. I
prefer to use foil instead of just the baking dish lid that does not
seal completely. Place in the preheated oven. Bake for 30 minutes.
Remove from oven. Stir well. If the rice is not done, return to oven,
covered well, for another 15 minutes. If, when you check the rice after
30 minutes, you find that the liquid is gone, add another 1/2 c. of
vegetable stock. Stir. Return to oven. This dish can also be kicked
up a notch by adding some form of chili peppers or cayenne pepper.

Orange Garlic Rice (V)

1 c. white or brown rice
2 c. orange juice (fresh, frozen, or mandarin orange juice from the canned mandarin oranges) (remember, some orange juice drinks contain sugar or a sweetener—read the label)
1 tbls. garlic (fresh, dried, or powdered)
1 tsp. KS
1 tsp. FGBP
1 c. green onions or dried chives

Here again, I like to cook this dish in the oven. If you have a smaller toaster oven, that is perfect. If you want to cook this rice dish on the stove top, that works also. I like the oven because I do not need to check it or worry if it is burning.

If you use the oven method, spray a 2 qt. baking dish well with pan spray. Boy, she sure likes to use pan spray! Yes, I do—it saves a lot of scrubbing. I also use it for anything I bake in the oven, such as pasta dishes or potato dishes. Okay, you have your baking dish sprayed, I suppose you are wondering, *Why a 2 qt. baking dish?* Rice doubles in size and needs room to grow without spilling over. If you use canned frozen orange juice, I like to use 3/4 the amount of water the directions call for. You can also use citrus fruit juices that include a variety of citrus juices. If I squeeze fresh oranges, I like to use the pulp also; it adds to the texture of the dish. If you like mandarin orange juice, by all means, use that, and do not be afraid to add some of the mandarin orange sections. If you cook for people that do not mind garlic if they do not see it in the finished product, use powdered. I have even known cooks that will use garlic juice in some recipes. Rice does tend to need a little more salt. I am not a big salt user, but sometimes I add extra to rice. Do not be afraid to. If you want to really taste the pepper in this dish, use more than what I recommend. Green onions or dried chives? Depends on what you have on hand or prefer. I like either.

If you use green onions, slice them all the way from the tip to the root end. Some cooks like to use only the green part. Not me! I use it all, sliced very thin. The flavor of dried chives really comes out when you cook with them. As in the other recipes, preheat the oven to 350 degrees. Combine everything together in the baking dish you have sprayed. Seal tightly with foil. Cook for 30 minutes. Remove from oven. Check for doneness. Add more liquid if needed (1/2 c.). Stir. Cover with the foil again. Return to oven for 15 minutes.

This rice dish is great served with chicken or pork. In fact, chicken can be placed on top of the rice mix, covered with foil, and baked. Same with pork chops or pork tenderloin. And YES, do not be afraid to add crushed red chilies or jalapeños.

Beef, Fish, Chicken, Turkey, and Pork

Duo of Bacon-Wrapped Grilled Beef Medallions with Roasted Garlic Cream Sauce

2 ea. 4 oz. beef medallions
2 ea. strips of thin-sliced bacon
Toothpicks (to secure bacon wrapped around beef)
1/4 c. roasted garlic cloves (recipe follows)
2 tbls. butter
1 c. heavy cream
1/2 tsp. KS
1/2 tsp. FGBP

 Beef? What kind of beef? Do I need to use an expensive cut? No, you don't! Talk to your butcher at the grocery where you shop about less expensive cuts such as chuck, rump roast, and round steak. The 4 oz. cut of meat doesn't have to be 2–3 inches thick. 1 inch, in my opinion, is plenty thick enough. I prefer to use thick-sliced bacon to wrap the beef in; it holds up better and doesn't cook away. Wrap the bacon around the beef medallions. Secure with a toothpick (do not forget to remove before serving). The beef can be cooked completely on the grill or marked off on a hot grill or flat top then finished in the oven. If you finish in the oven, use a 400-degree oven. Place beef in a baking dish or pie pan. Add some liquid of some sort—beef stock, white wine, or beer work great. For rare, I would recommend cooking all the way on the grill. For medium, if you finish in oven, this may take 5–8 minutes; well done, about 10 minutes. I prefer to cook completely on the grill.

Bacon-Wrapped Meatloaf
with Mushroom Au Jus

1 lb. ground beef, ground turkey, ground chicken or 1/2 ground
beef, 1/2 ground pork (the choice is yours)
8 slices of bacon
1/2 c. finely diced onion
1/2 c. bread crumbs
2 ea. eggs
1/2 tsp. KS
1 tsp. FGBP
1 tbls. Worcestershire sauce
2 tsp. chopped garlic
Baking dish
Pan spray

Preheat the oven to 350 degrees. In a mixing bowl, add the meat.
Finely dice the onion, then add to meat. Add the bread crumbs, eggs,
salt, and pepper, and to taste Worcestershire sauce and chopped
garlic. Mix well. Lay out 4 strips of bacon, separated. Take 1/2 the
meatloaf mix, shape round or oval, and place on top of 2 slices
of bacon. Fold bacon over. It can be secured with toothpicks, if
you prefer. Wrap the other slices of bacon the other directions.
Secure with toothpicks, if you prefer. Spray baking dish well.
Place meatloaves in the dish. Place in oven for 1 hour. Remove
from oven. Let rest 5 minutes before removing from baking dish
to serve. This meatloaf can be made 2–3 days ahead. Remove
from fridge 30 minutes before baking to warm up. If going from
fridge to oven, add an extra 10–15 minutes on baking time.

Swedish Meatballs

1 lb. ground beef
1/2 lb. ground pork or sausage
1 c. white onion
2 ea. whole eggs
1 c. bread crumbs
1 tbls. Italian seasoning
1 tbls. garlic
1 tsp. KS
2 tsp. FGBP

In a mixing bowl, combine the meats, bread crumbs, Italian seasoning, salt, and pepper. In a blender or processor, combine the peeled and chopped-up onion, garlic, and eggs. Blend well. Add to meat mixture. Mix everything together well. Preheat oven to 350 degrees. Shape meat mixture into size meatballs desired. Place in baking dish. Bake for 15 to 20 minutes or until done. Remove from pan out of grease into another baking dish. Cover with Swedish meatball sauce. Return to oven for about 30 minutes. These meatballs are great served with pasta, rice, or potatoes, along with a green vegetable, such as green beans or broccoli.

Country-Fried Steak

2 ea. 6 oz. cube steak or round steak
1/2 c. flour
1/2 tsp. KS
1 tsp. FGBP
1 tsp. garlic powder
1 tsp. onion powder
1 c. EVOO or salad oil
1 ea. can pan spray
1 ea. skillet
2 c. beef gravy (the recipe for beef gravy is in the **Sauces and Au Jus** section, or use the directions for the pan gravy in this recipe)

If you purchase round steak, you will need to pound with a meat-tenderizer mallet.

> *Cube steak, or minute steak, as they call it in some stores, is from the top or bottom round, cut into portion size, then run through a tenderizing machine 1 or 2 times. If this is not done, the meat would be too tough to eat. You do not need to pound the meat to tenderize it if you buy cube steaks.*

To do this, cut the round steak into 6 oz. pieces. In a shallow dish, mix flour (just enough to coat the steak pieces) with the garlic powder, onion powder, KS, and FGBP. Coat each side well. Use either a ziplock bag, plastic wrap, or wax paper. If using ziplock, just place flour-coated meat inside the bag. If using plastic wrap or wax paper, put meat between 2 sheets. Use the mallet to pound away on both sides of the meat until it is well pounded and all the fibers are broken up.

If you use already-processed cube steak, just dredge in the flour mix well on both sides. Put the skillet on medium heat. Let get hot, but not too hot. Add the oil. Make sure it doesn't smoke. If it smokes, it's too hot. Turn off. Let cool. Wipe with paper towel. Start again. Place the meat in the hot skillet. Brown well on 1 side. Flip over; let finish cooking until done. Add the gravy. Let simmer for about 10 minutes. Turn off heat. Place meat on plate with mashed potatoes. Cover both with the hot gravy. If you are using the pan drippings to make the gravy (in my opinion, this is the only way to do it), you need equal amounts of drippings and flour. If there isn't enough pan drippings, add more oil. Just a little! You will need maybe 1/4 c. total of drippings and flour. When the drippings are hot, add 1/4 c. of flour. Mix well with a whisk and keep stirring until thick and dry. Slowly add 2 c. water or beef broth, stirring constantly until you have the consistency you want. This will be different from the beef gravy made with roux and broth in the **Sauces and Au Jus** section of this book.

Fish or Chicken Cooked in a Paper Sack with Vegetables

2 ea. paper lunch sacks
1 ea. stapler (optional) or 6 ea. metal paper clips
2 ea. 6 oz. fish filets (fresh or frozen)
2 ea. 6 oz. chicken breasts or thighs
1 ea. onion (white, yellow, or red)
1 ea. large, whole, fresh carrot
1 ea. large zucchini or 2 ea. small zucchini
2 tbls. dill (fresh or dried) or 2 tbls. thyme or rosemary (fresh or dried)
1/2 tsp. KS
1 tsp. FGBP
1 ea. fresh lemon
1 ea. cookie sheet

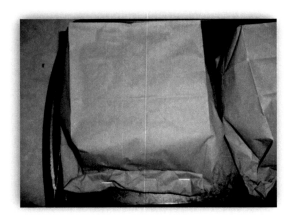

En papillote (pah-pee-YOHT; pah-peh-loht): This term refers to food cooked in greased parchment paper and is a French term and common in French cooking. The food steams inside the paper, then is served table side in the

parchment, cut open, and food is eaten out of the pouch. In this recipe, I use paper sacks.

Preheat oven to 350 degrees. Cut the onion, zucchini, and carrots into julienne slices (thin, matchstick slices). Slice the lemon into 4 pieces. In the paper bags, place the fish filets or chicken. Top with the vegetables, KS and FGBP, lemon slices, 1 tbls. water, and dill. Seal up really well (fold under 3 times) so steam doesn't escape. A stapler may be used to seal the bags well, or 3 metal paper clips. Place on a cookie sheet in the oven. Bake for 12 minutes. To serve, place bags on a dinner plate. Cut open carefully so you don't get burned by the steam. If you prefer, the filets can be removed from the bags and carefully placed on plates. Make sure to dump the juice on the fish. This dish is great when served with a simple rice dish.

Grilled or Baked Salmon with Spiced Mandarin Oranges

2 ea. salmon filets
1 c. spiced mandarin oranges (recipe in the **Relishes and Condiments** section)
1/2 tsp. KS
1 tsp. FGBP
2 c. orange garlic rice (recipe in the **Potatoes, Pasta, and Rice** section)

Should I grill the salmon? If I grill it, should I use wood, charcoal, or gas? Should I add wood chips to smoke the salmon? The directions to smoke food is in the recipe for **Smoked or Roasted Red Onion Red Bell Pepper**. Or should I bake the salmon? Should I grill it or bake it with skin on or off? I prefer to do skin off, generously salting and peppering both sides. When I grill fish, I always like to spray both sides with pan spray well. Fish sticks really badly to the grill, especially if you do not have a really hot grill. If you like a nice diamond mark on your fish, chicken, steak, or pork, when you grill find the hottest part of the grill and lay the fish straight across. Let cook desired time (for fish about 3 minutes), then carefully turn halfway so it is straight up and down on grill to finish cooking on that side, then flip over and do the same thing with that side. This will create a beautiful diamond design. If straight grill marks are your liking, then cook on each side until done, turning one time.

If you like to bake your salmon, preheat the oven to 350 degrees. Generously spray a baking pan. Coat each side with the salt and pepper. Place in the baking dish. I like to add about 1/4 c. white wine or some of the liquid from the spiced mandarin oranges, then place in the oven. Bake for 8 to 12 minutes. To plate this dish, use dinner plates. Place half the orange garlic rice in the center of each plate, then top with the salmon. Place half of the spiced mandarin oranges on top of the salmon. If you are grilling the salmon, why not grill some asparagus or zucchini along with it? If you are baking the salmon, why not sauté bell peppers, onions, and zucchini to serve with the salmon? Chicken or pork are also great served with the **Spiced Mandarin Oranges** and **Orange Garlic Rice**.

Rosemary Roasted Chicken Quarters with Roasted Red Bell Pepper Sauce

4 ea. chicken quarters (white or dark meat, skin on)
1/4 c. rosemary leaves (fresh or dried)
2 tbls. fresh garlic (chopped)
4 tbls. butter
1 tsp. KS
2 tsp. FGBP
1 c. roasted red bell pepper sauce (recipe in the **Sauces and Au Jus** section)

*Rosemary is a mint-family herb used since 500 BC. It grows wild all through the Mediterranean and parts of the southwest United States. The needle-shaped, silvery-green leaves are very aromatic with scents of lemon and mint. It is used in all areas of cooking: for example, in fruit salads, entree salads, soups, sauces, stews, and roasting. It can be purchased fresh, dried, or powdered.

I like to use the hindquarters (legs and thighs with part of the back attached; in other words, dark meat). To start this dish, preheat the oven to 400 degrees. Rinse off the chicken. Dry with a paper towel. I carefully loosen the skin from the meat all the way to the end of the leg. Soften the butter in a mixing bowl, but do not melt it. Mix the chopped garlic, butter, KS, FGBP, and rosemary together. Using my hands, I carefully lift up the skin, spread the butter mix over the meat under the skin, and use it all. Place the chicken in a baking dish sprayed well with pan spray. I suggest using a baking rack so the chicken is not sitting in the grease. Place this in the preheated oven. Cook for 30 minutes, or until internal temperature is 160 degrees. The proper way to use a meat thermometer on chicken hindquarters is to insert the probe end of the thermometer into the flesh part of the leg. Do not touch the bone; you will get a false reading. The skin should be crisp and golden brown. The **Roasted Red Bell Pepper Sauce** can be served over the chicken or on the side for dipping. I like to serve either mashed potatoes or roasted potatoes with this chicken dish. The mashed potatoes can be made with sundried tomatoes blended in or potatoes roasted with the chicken.

Cherry Chicken

2 ea. 6 oz. chicken breasts
1 c. cherry sauce (recipe in the **Sauces and Au Jus** section)

Clean and remove all fat from the chicken breast. Grill or bake until done. Place on a dinner plate. Top with the cherry sauce. A twice-baked potato is very good served with this chicken dish. Also, green beans are a great vegetable served with this chicken.

Grilled Chicken with Feta Cheese, Olives, and Rosemary

2 ea. 6 oz. chicken breasts or 2 ea. legs with thighs (skin on)
1 c. feta cheese, olives, and rosemary (the recipe for **Feta Cheese and Olives with Rosemary** is in the **Relishes and Condiments** section)
1 tsp. KS
1 tsp. FGBP

This recipe is very short and simple to make. All you have to do is decide what pieces of chicken you want: breasts or legs or thighs; also, what you want to grill your chicken over: gas grill, charcoal, or wood. We grill only on wood—apple and cherry, to be exact. If you like to marinate your chicken, I suggest just using oil, EVOO, or vegetable oil with garlic, KS, and FGBP only. The chicken can be marinated in this for several days. If you add an acid such as vinegar or fruit juice, you cannot marinate more than 6 hours because the acid will start to cook the meat. The feta cheese, olives, and rosemary can be taken out of the oven several hours before use to warm up to room temperature. Grill the chicken of choice the way you want it, then place on large dinner plates. Top with the feta cheese, olives, and rosemary, or serve the feta cheese, olives, and rosemary on the side to top each bite. I also suggest serving a baked potato with butter and sour cream or the **Rice Primavera** with this chicken dish.

Turkey Divan

4 ea. slices of roasted turkey breast, 6 inches long, 1/4 inch thick
2 ea. crowns of broccoli
1 c. Mornay sauce (recipe in the **Sauces and Au Jus** section)
1 tsp. KS
1 tsp. FGBP

Broccoli crowns? What are broccoli crowns? They are the cluster of broccoli florets just above the stem. To make this dish, you will need to preheat the oven to 350 degrees and, yes, spray a baking dish with pan spray. Put a pot of water with plenty of KS in it on the stove. Let come to a boil. Cut the broccoli cluster of florets off of the stem. Cut this into 4 pieces the long way. In a small pot on the stove, have the Mornay sauce ready and hot. Lay the 4 slices of turkey breast on a flat surface. When the water comes to a boil on the stove, drop in the broccoli. Let blanch for about 5 minutes. Remove from the pot. Drain; do not rinse. Using tongs, lay 2 pieces of broccoli on each slice of turkey breast at one end with florets facing out. Sprinkle with the KS and FGBP. Roll up. Lay in baking dish. Continue until you have 4 roll-ups. Top with the Mornay sauce. Place in the oven. Let bake for 30 minutes. Remove from oven. Place 2 roll-ups on each plate. Serve with potatoes, rice, or a pasta dish of your choice.

Roast Pork Loin with Rhubarb Sauce

5 lbs. pork loin
1 tbls. KS
1 tbls. FGBP
1 c. rhubarb sauce (recipe in the **Sauces and Au Jus** section)

This is another simple, easy-to-make recipe. The pork loin you purchase may have a layer of fat on one side; this can be removed or left on. If you leave it on the loin, roast fat-side up so the fat juices go into the loin. The end result will be much more tender and juicy. Why 5 lbs.? This allows for shrinkage, and you will want extra for another meal. Yes, you can use a smaller pork loin. You can also grill it instead of roasting.

To roast, preheat oven to 450 degrees. I like to mix the KS and FGBP together then generously rub into the pork loin. Any herbs you like can also be used for the rub: rosemary, thyme, Italian seasoning, garlic, and onion powder, just to name a few. There are no herbs in the rhubarb sauce, but that does not mean you cannot add some to the sauce or the pork loin. Let the pork loin sit out at room temperature for 30 minutes to take the chill off. If you are roasting, I suggest you use a roasting rack with the roasting pan. Yes, use pan spray generously before putting the loin in the pan, with or without a rack. The reason I use a rack is that way the meat is not sitting in the grease but will still be moist and juicy. Yes, you can add the pan drippings to the rhubarb sauce for more flavor—I recommend that you do this.

To roast, place the loin in the pan in the 450-degree, preheated oven. Let roast on 450 for 30 minutes. This seals in the juices and also crisps the fat cap. Turn the oven down to 300 degrees. Cook for 2 hours. Use a meat thermometer to check roasting temperature. When the internal temperature is 165 degrees, the pork loin is done. I am a believer that pork needs to be well done to kill any bacteria that grows in pork. Chicken should also be well done. No one wants salmonella.

Salmonella (sal-muh-NEHL-uh) is a very nasty bacteria that enters the body through contaminated food or water, especially meats, poultry, and cracked eggshells. It has no smell, taste, or signs it is there. It takes 6 to 8 hours or as much as 3 days to show up. The symptoms are diarrhea, stomach pain, nausea, vomiting, headache, fever, and chills. Death is very rare but can happen. On the good side, antibiotics can take care of it. So, make sure you cook pork and chicken very well. When buying eggs, make sure there are not cracked shells. A lot of people wash their eggs in cold water and store in another container.

When the loin has reached 165 degrees, remove from the oven. Let rest for 30 minutes either in the pan or on a cutting board. Slice to your desired thickness. Place as many slices as you like on dinner plates. Drizzle with the rhubarb sauce or serve the sauce on the side. As with most of my sauces, you can add some spice, such as cayenne pepper or jalapeños. For a smoky flavor, use chipotle chilies (dried, smoked jalapeños in adobo sauce). Serve this pork loin with a vegetable and starch of your choice. I have served with egg noodles used for the starch. I cook the noodles then toss lightly in EVOO, place in the center of the dinner plates, and top with the rhubarb sauce. Peas can also be tossed with the noodles.

Stuffed Baked Pork Chops
with Green Tomato Sauce

2 ea. 1-inch-thick pork chops
1 tsp. KS
1 tsp. FGBP
1–2 c. corn bread stuffing (recipe follows)
1 c. green tomato sauce (recipe in the **Sauces and Au Jus** section)

Pork again? Yes, pork again! You can also use the pork loin to make this. In fact, the pork loin is the pork chops with the bone removed. Any meat department at any store will be happy to cut you 1-inch pork chops. When you get them home and are ready to cook, leave them to sit out at room temperature for 30 minutes before cooking. As in the pork loin recipe, I like to use a baking rack. Preheat the oven to 450 degrees.

Use a paring knife to cut the pork chops in the center so you can stuff them. Cut all the way through to the bone. Coat both sides with the KS and FGBP. Fill with the stuffing. Place in pan on rack. If your roasting pan has a lid, put it on. If not, cover well with foil. Roast for 30 minutes. Turn the oven down to 300 degrees. Let cook at least 2 hours, until center is 165 degrees.

The reason I cover the pan is because the steam helps cook the stuffing. You want to make sure the stuffing is well done since it is made with raw egg. Remove from the oven. Place on dinner plates. Drizzle with green tomato sauce or serve on side. If you do not like to stuff chops but like pork chops and stuffing, place the chops on top of the stuffing in a baking dish sprayed. Cover with foil. Cook for 30 minutes on 450. Turn heat down to 300. Cook another 2 hours. Make sure you check internal temperature with a meat thermometer.

Corn Bread

1/4 c. butter or margarine
1 c. buttermilk
1 ea. white egg
1 1/4 c. cornmeal (white or yellow)
1 c. flour
1/2 c. sugar
1 tbls. baking powder
1/2 tsp. KS
1 ea. 9 x 1 1/2 round or 8 x 8 x 2 square baking pan
Pan spray

Kosher salt in baking? Is that not a no-no? To some it is, to me it is not. I am not a professional baker, but I can bake. I also prefer to use buttermilk for corn bread, biscuits, and pancakes. It just adds that something to the taste. White or yellow cornmeal: the choice is yours. To me, corn bread just does not look like corn bread if it is white. Yellow cornmeal is made of yellow corn kernels that are dried and ground. White cornmeal is from white kernels of corn that are smaller and sweeter than yellow corn. If you have not used white cornmeal but would like to try it, I suggest tasting the white cornmeal before adding sugar, or make a batch then adjust the sugar amount. If it is too sweet, maybe use 1/3 c.

Preheat the oven to 400 degrees. Measure then combine all the ingredients together in a mixing bowl. Mixture should be thick and have some lumps. Pour into the baking dish of your choice. Bake for 20 to 25 minutes until golden brown. This corn bread is great with almost everything. The recipe makes more than you will need for the stuffing.

Corn Bread Stuffing

1 c. cooked, dried corn bread
1 c. dried bread crumbs (white, wheat, French, Italian, sourdough)
1 tbls. dried sage
2 ea. whole eggs
1 c. broth (pork, vegetable, or chicken)
1/2 c. celery
1/2 c. onion (white or yellow)
1 tsp. KS
1 tsp. FGBP
2 tbls. butter

To make this stuffing, dry the corn bread and other bread. This can be done by letting the bread sit out at room temperature or put in the oven on 250 for several hours. The bread can also be used without drying. I like the stuffing results better with the breads dried. You can also buy already-dried stuffing mix.

Dice the celery small (I like to use the leaves also; they are full of flavor). Dice the onion small. Melt the butter in a saucepan. Add the celery and onion. Sauté until tender. Add the KS, FGBP, sage, and broth. Let simmer for about 30 minutes. Turn off the heat. Let cool down (if you do not and pour it right on the eggs in the mixing bowl, the eggs will cook). In a mixing bowl, add the dried breads and eggs. Pour on the cooled broth mix. Using your hands or a spoon, mix well, then taste for sage, KS, and FGBP. Add more if needed. Dried fruit can also be added to this stuffing for a sweet treat. Stuff the pork chops. Bake. Enjoy.

Bacon Egg Potato Pie

1 ea. deep-dish pie crust in pie pan
2 c. sliced potatoes (white bakers, red skin, Yukon gold, etc.)
1 pkg. thin-sliced bacon
1 ea. onion (white or yellow)
2 tbls. KS
1 tbls. FGBP
6 ea. whole eggs
1/2 c. milk, heavy cream, or half-and-half
2 c. shredded cheese (your choice; any flavor works)

    I do not make good pie shells, so I buy them premade and frozen. I do not give a recipe to make pie shells. Preheat the oven to 350 degrees. Wash the potatoes and slice very thin. It is up to you if you want to peel them; I do not and they cook just fine. Take the bacon from the package. Cut down the center, making each slice into 2. Peel and slice the onion thinly. Crack the eggs. Add the KS and FGBP along with the milk. Whip together well. Using the pie shell in a pie pan, layer the potatoes, onions, and cheese. Last is bacon (I go in around the pie shell with the bacon center out). Use half of the ingredients for the first layer, then the other half for the second layer. I finish with the last layer of bacon on top, so when it bakes you have this nice, crunchy bacon on top. Using a fork, slowly lift the potatoes around the edges a little at a time. Pour the egg mixture in. It will go down through the layers. If you pour it over the top, it will just run all off. It needs to get down into the layers. Place in the preheated oven. Bake for 1 hour and 30 minutes. It is done when a knife inserted in the center comes out clean. Other foods such as sausage, bell peppers, or mushrooms can be added or used instead. Serve this dish with a side of fresh fruit and crusty bread. Yummy!

Desserts

Bread Pudding (V)

4 c. bread chunks
4 ea. whole eggs
Milk to cover bread chunks
1/4 c. sugar
1 tbls. ground cinnamon
1 ea. stick of butter
1 c. nuts (optional)
1 c. raisins (optional)
1 c. chocolate caramel sauce (optional) (recipe follows)

In a large bowl, add bread. (This is a way to use up old hamburger buns, hot dog buns, cinnamon rolls, biscuits, etc.) Add whole eggs, sugar, cinnamon, nuts, and raisins, if desired. Cover all with milk. Let set for at least 2 hours. Overnight in the fridge is ideal. Use a hand mixer or stand mixer to blend well. If you want it chunky, do not use mixer; just mix by hand. Preheat oven to 350 degrees. Spray individual baking dishes or one big enough to hold all the mixture. Pour mixture into baking dishes. Slice the butter into pieces about 1/4 inch thick. Place on top of bread pudding. For individual dishes, add 2–3 slices. For one big dish, add all the butter. Place in oven. Bake for 60 to 90 minutes. Serve warm with chocolate caramel sauce.

Bread pudding was a favorite of my brothers, sister, and I for breakfast. Our mom would make several cake pans of it. We ate it hot as soon as it came out of the oven and for breakfast the next day. She would heat a skillet, add butter to melt, slice the bread pudding, place in the skillet, brown with the butter, then sprinkle with sugar to eat.

Chocolate Caramel Sauce (V)

Sauté pan
1 ea. stick butter
1 c. sugar
1 c. heavy cream
1 c. chocolate chips

In a sauté pan on medium heat, add butter. Stir constantly. When melted, add sugar. Stir constantly until sugar melts and turns golden brown. Add heavy cream and chocolate chips. Stir until thick and chocolate chips are melted. Turn off heat. Serve warm over bread pudding.

Baked Pears (V)

2 ea. fresh pears
2 tbls. blue cheese (or your choice of cheese)
2 tbls. nuts (your choice)
2 scoops of vanilla ice cream (or your choice of ice cream)
Balsamic syrup (your choice of flavor)

Preheat oven to 350 degrees. Spray a baking dish. Wash and cut in half each pear. Remove stem and strings inside pear halves. Use a spoon or melon baller to remove some of the meat from inside the pear, leaving a hole to fill with cheese (maybe 1/2 inch round and deep). Do not go all the way through to the skin on the bottom of the hole. Place the pears in the baking dish. Top with the cheese and nuts. Place in oven. Check after 10 minutes. The cheese should be melting and bubbly. The baking dishes you use can be individual for each serving to make easier to handle. Remove from oven. If using individual baking dishes, top with ice cream and drizzle with balsamic. Enjoy! If using large baking dish, carefully remove, placing 2 on each serving dish. Top with ice cream and balsamic drizzle.

Spice Cake (V)

1 small white or yellow cake mix
1 tsp. ground cinnamon
1 tsp. ground cloves
1 tsp. ground nutmeg
1/2 c. chopped nuts (your choice) (I suggest walnuts)
1/2 c. chopped raisins, dates, or both
1 ea. 8 in. cake pan
1 ea. canned cream-cheese frosting mix (or frosting of your choice, or if you prefer, sprinkle powdered sugar)

Preheat oven according to directions on cake-mix box. Combine all the ingredients. Mix well. Spray pan really well with pan spray. Pour in cake mix. Bake according to directions. Remove from oven when done. Let completely cool in the pan or on a baking rack. When completely cooled, place on serving platter. Frost generously with frosting of your choice. More nuts and/or raisins can be added to garnish.

Peach Cobbler (V)

4 c. peaches (fresh, frozen, or canned)
1/2 c. cinnamon and brown sugar mix (4 tbls. cinnamon, 4 tbls.
brown sugar. If you think that is too much cinnamon for you,
go 3 tbls. cinnamon to 4 tbls. brown sugar. Artificial brown sugar
can be used. It is very good.)
4 c. rolled oats
4 tbls. butter
1 ea. 8 in. baking dish or 2 individual baking dishes

Preheat oven to 350 degrees. Spray the baking dishes well with
pan spray. If using frozen peaches, let thaw completely. If not, this
will add 20 minutes or more to baking time. Place the peaches in
the baking dishes. Sprinkle with half of the cinnamon and brown
sugar mix. Melt the butter. Put in a mixing bowl. Add the oatmeal
and other half of cinnamon and brown sugar mix. Blend together
well. Spread over peaches. Place in oven for 30 minutes. If top is
not browned and crunchy with the peaches bubbling, let cook
another 10 minutes. Remove from oven. Enjoy.

Pound Cake with Peaches, Pears, and Raisins Soaked in Spiced Rum Sauce (V)

4 ea. 1/2-inch slices of pound cake (any variety)
1 c. peaches (canned or jarred, fresh or frozen; spiced are really good)
1 c. pears (canned, jarred, or fresh; spiced are really good)
1/2 c. raisins (regular or golden; soaked in spiced rum optional)
1 c. spiced rum sauce (recipe follows)
Whipped cream
2 ea. dessert plates

Store-bought pound cake? I have tried to keep these recipes simple. There are some good premade pound cakes out there in the freezer section of the grocery stores. They are nice to keep on hand for fast desserts. Spiced peaches and pears? Never heard of them. My Grandma Ikie used to make her own. Of course, she had peach and pear trees in her yard. If you like to can, buy them in season. When you put them in the jars, add a cinnamon stick, nutmeg, and fresh or ground cloves before putting on the lids and rings. Then cook. If you are using regular canned or jarred, open the jar lid, add the spicing ingredients, close the lid, and put in the fridge for at least a week. If you use frozen, make a simple syrup (equal amounts of sugar and water heated until sugar is dissolved with the spicing ingredients; let cool before using). Put the frozen fruit in a container you can seal. Pour the simple syrup over the frozen fruit. Seal and cover. Put in the fridge for a week. They should be eaten within 3 weeks, as they will mold. So, I suggest only make what you need. They are so easy to make. A lot of specialty stores carry spiced canned peaches and pears. Some of the spiced rum can be added to these when you refrigerate them, as well as the raisins can be added. The raisins can also be put in a container with rum added, then put in the fridge for a week. Make sure the kids do not find them. I suggest dessert plates for this.

Slice the pound cake into 1/2-inch slices. Place 2 slices on each plate. Pour 2 tbls. of the rum sauce over each slice. Top that with the peaches, pears, and raisins, then top with the whipped cream, then drizzle another 2 tbls. of the rum sauce over it all. A sprig of fresh mint or chopped nuts can be added to garnish. Of course, berries can be used to make this dessert instead or added with. If you do not like raisins, then use dried cranberries or other dried fruit instead.

Spiced Rum Sauce

2 c. spiced rum (any brand)
1 tbls. cornstarch
2 tbls. water

This sauce is very simple to make. In a saucepan, add the spiced rum. If you know how to flame the rum without getting hurt, you can. I do not do that; I just heat up the rum on low heat. Mix the cornstarch with the water. Mix together. Stir into the rum until dissolved. Let simmer for about 5 minutes. Serve hot over the pound cake and fruit.

The raisins can also be added to the rum sauce instead of with the fruit, or marinated in the rum alone. Then this becomes raisin rum sauce. That is also very good served over bread pudding. This sauce will store nicely in the fridge for a long time, but it will not last that long. The use for it is endless: over ice cream, bread pudding, apple pie, peach pie, or pecan pie, for just a few suggestions.

S'mores Parfait (V)

Chocolate sauce
Marshmallow cream
Graham cracker crumbs
Glasses (any style you choose)

I do not give quantities for this recipe because it depends on how much of what you like. I like to use tall wine glasses. Of course, this requires iced-tea spoons to reach all the goodness.

I start by putting some chocolate sauce in the bottom, then a layer of graham crackers, then marshmallow cream, then more chocolate sauce, continuing to layer to your satisfaction, ending with a generous squirt of chocolate sauce and maybe a maraschino cherry on top.

Filo Cups Filled with Strawberries and Chocolate (V)

10 ea. filo dough cups
10 ea. chocolate drops
5 ea. fresh strawberries
1 pkg. filo dough or 1 box premade frozen filo cups
1 cookie sheet
1 small muffin pan
1 stick melted butter

Make sure the filo dough is not frozen. If it is, let thaw at least 1 hour before handling. Preheat the oven to 350 degrees. Filo dough is very delicate and paper thin. When working with filo dough, keep the pile of dough covered with a damp (not wet) cloth. Between working with layers, it dries out very fast and gets crumbly.

Melt the butter. Be careful not to burn. On a clean, dry surface, lay one sheet of filo dough after carefully unrolling the stack of dough. Lay one sheet on the clean, dry surface. Brush well and carefully with the melted butter. Add another sheet of filo dough. Brush well and carefully with melted butter. Do this 3 more times, making 5 layers. Use a pizza cutter or sharp knife to cut filo into 6 pieces. Place the 6 pieces of filo dough into the muffin pan. Bake for 5 minutes at 350 degrees or until golden brown. Do not overcook. They will be put back into the oven with strawberries and chocolate. Cut the strawberries into 6 slices ea. Place 3 slices around the inside edges of the filo dough in the muffin pan. Add the chocolate drop. Place in preheated, 350-degree oven for 5 minutes or until chocolate melts. Oven temperatures vary; some may take 5 minutes, some 8 or 10.

Remove from oven. Let sit 2 minutes. Carefully remove from the muffin pan to serving plates. Drizzle with strawberry or chocolate balsamic vinegar, if desired. If you are using premade, prebaked filo cups, place on a cookie sheet, fill with strawberries and chocolate, and bake.

About the Author

Janie Ebinger is a wife, mother, and grandmother who is very passionate about her family and food. She had a long career cooking. She felt like a sponge in that she could not learn enough, fast enough. She enjoys teaching cooking classes and sharing new foods with others.

Other Books by Janie Ebinger

Simply Vinaigrettes: From Ancho Chili to White Wine

Janie's Simply Entree Salads for Two

Live Well Eat Well:
Janie's Twist on Salads, Sandwiches, and Wraps